Libby James

Still Running

One step at a time

Also by Libby James

Muffin Magic
Frisbee Dreams
Running Mates
White Shadow

Libby James

ISBN-10: 0-9968819-6-4
ISBN-13: 978-0-9668819-6-8

Library of Congress Control Number
2018947036

Penstemon Pubications
Wellington, Colorado

For Dave Klibbe, who is
always ready to go for a run.

Libby James

Contents

Libby James

Still Running

Introduction

Snow began falling on the Friday before the 1978 Denver Marathon. Flakes descended quietly and persisted through the night. By morning the world was white and the flakes were still falling. On Sunday morning I was due in Denver at the starting line for my first attempt at a full marathon--26.2 miles. I was 42 years old and knew little about the running world. I did not know how that day would change my life, I only knew that it was snowing. And that I would be by myself. My training partner lived high in the foothills above Fort Collins, several miles off a paved road. Late Saturday when I spoke to her she was snowed in. "This cannot be," I remember saying. "It's May!"

"I can plod through the snow on foot for four miles to the road," she replied, "But there's no way I'd be able to run 26 miles after that." She was headed for the liquor cabinet.

I ran the race alone. The temperature was 29 degrees at the start. The streets were filled with slush but the sun was shining and the temperature rose as time went by. When

I finished, three hours and forty-eight minutes later, I felt terrible for about ten minutes. And then I was overcome by a totally new sensation. If I could run 26.2 miles and finish standing up, then I could do anything! Perhaps not entirely rational, but 40 years later I'm still running. I suspect it may have something to do with completing that first marathon. Note: The organizers of the Denver Marathon have not scheduled the race for early May since that memorable year.

I'd been running for more than five years but only competing in races for two. That day began a voyage of discovery that continues to this day. Running has changed. Our bodies have changed. The culture around running, especially for women, has changed. I have reached an age group where I often have no competition. There are usually a few men. I have to fess up that I find it quite gratifying to outrun the men in my age group. And mostly they are gracious losers.

The older you get, the harder it is to run. You can't go as far or as fast. But you can still go. It still makes me feel good to work up enough sweat to earn a shower. Most times, it is not the adrenalin produced by entering a race that keeps me going, it is the comfortably familiar repetition of a daily run.

During the last four decades, I've spent a good bit of time thinking about the sport of running, coming to appreciate its many benefits and the opportunities it has provided me for going places, getting to know wonderful people, learning about how to eat better, and giving me quiet time to think. Through years of regular running I've learned to do it more efficiently and how to avoid getting injured.

I have learned to appreciate the egalitarian nature of the sport of running. I've formed some of my closest friendships while on the move. In the words of a running friend, "Running is the only sport where the elite— the champions—participate in races at the same time and in the same place as rank beginners—sometimes even with dogs and strollers--and everyone else in between."

That's one of the things I love about this simplest of all sports. It is the lowly act of putting one foot in front of the other and doing it over and over again. It is no more than a hyped-up version of walking, the most elemental and necessary of human movements. Scientists speculate that human beings could run before they could think. Instinct told them to run, to chase after food and to escape from danger.

I came to running when I was well beyond what would have been my prime running years. I've never been sorry about that though. Never having been a runner in high school and college, I really don't know what I missed or how fast I might have been. There was no *personal best* in my past to compete with as I grew older.

By the time I ran the first mile in my neighborhood when I was 35, just to see if I could do it, I was already on the downhill side of the game. Yet, with practice, I was able to increase my speed and the pleasure I felt when running. I ran my fastest marathon when I was 47 which inspired me to keep at it. Some of the best runners I've known have become discouraged when the passage of time slows them down. When forced to confront reality and be comfortable with slower times, they quit. Uncooperative backs, hips, ankles and especially knees often forced them to put an end to their running days.

I admit to a period of time early on when I put in a couple thousand miles a year. I ran a marathon every six months or so and did lots of half marathons and shorter races as well. It was when I got over that fanatic phase that I began to appreciate the joy of this sport that I had discovered, almost by accident.

For several years I wrote a monthly column for our local newspaper. I never ran out of things to say about my favorite sport and I looked forward to sharing my thoughts with others. This book is a continuation of that effort. Many of the stories originally appeared in my column and now appear revised and updated. Others have been adapted from my blog, "AdLibs." All of them reflect my love of running and share the ways in which it has enriched my life.

I hope that readers, runners or not, will discover that they can relate to what I have to say. Maybe some will decide to lace up their shoes and hit the road, even if it is just for a jog around the block.

Are You *Still* Running?

It's a question I'm often asked, especially by people I haven't seen for a while. I understand that the question is a well-meant conversation opener, but I'm asked so often that I chuckle inside when I hear the question. There's a smartypants little voice inside my head that wants to respond with a wisecrack: *Are you still brushing your teeth?* But I don't. I just answer yes.

After more than four decades of hitting the road, I am still running and it has become as much a part of my day as brushing my teeth. I hope to keep at it until I can no longer hoist a toothbrush to my mouth. By then I suspect my legs will no longer be willing to carry me out the door, but if they will, I'll walk.

Long ago I met a 71-year-old woman at a local race. I was blown away by her ancient age—and by the wrinkly condition of her legs that looked just the way mine do now. I could not imagine someone that old competing in a race. That was a decade ago.

When I started to run in the early 1970s, I went out before the sun came up so that no one would see me. My four kids were approaching adolescence en masse, and life was a little crazy. I formed the habit of getting up just early enough to run a mile and get home in time to make breakfast, pack lunches and see everyone off to school. That

15-minute run became a treasured mental
health time for me. I enjoyed it so much that
after I turned 40 in 1976, I had upped my
mileage to the point where I thought I was
ready to enter a local 10k road race.

In those days there weren't many masters
(over 40) women runners around, at least
not in Fort Collins Colorado, a situation that
made my age group, women 40 to 44, quite
small. Among a few female competitors in a
race at City Park, a few blocks from my home,
my time of 44-plus minutes for 6.2 miles
looked pretty good. It inspired me enough to
contemplate attempting a full marathon, a
distance of 26.2 miles, originally determined
by the distance between Windsor Castle and
Buckingham Palace in the UK. I began to step
up my training miles. Two years later I wasn't
getting any younger, the popularity of
running had exploded, and I decided to give
the marathon a try.

Events like Kathrine Switzer's completion
of the "men only" Boston Marathon in 1967
and Frank Shorter's gold medal in the 1972
Olympic Marathon had inspired a running
boom in the U.S. and beyond. Kathrine, a
student at Syracuse University, had trained to
run the distance and used her initials to apply
for an official race number and pay her $3
fee. Nowhere was it written that women
were not allowed to enter the race officially.
She began the race with her coach and
boyfriend at her side. When someone on the
press truck noticed her, race director Jock
Semple jumped from the truck and tried to

tear off her race number. He was prevented from doing so by her boyfriend while a photographer caught the sequence on film. She finished the race as an official entrant with a time for four hours and twenty minutes and the running world was changed forever.

Inspired by Kathrine and runners like Frank Shorter, Bill Rodgers and Alberto Salazaar, running became increasingly popular. In 1974 a national marathon championship for women was established. Jock Semple saw the handwriting on the wall, admitted women to the Boston Marathon and later became good friends with Kathrine. But it took a decade to convince the Olympic Committee. In 1984, the women's marathon became an Olympic event and Joan Benoit (Samuelson) brought home the gold for the USA in Los Angeles.

The peak of my training regime before my first marathon was a 20-mile run on a flat one-mile stretch in a residential area close to my house, ten times out and ten times back. I was out there all morning. The neighbors were beginning to wonder.

I'm still running for lots of reasons: physical, social and psychological. I'm fortunate that my body allows me to run this late in life. I try not to punish my body too much, in the hope that it will continue to hold up. I thank my knees and feet, my back and my lungs for hanging in there with me. Running has influenced the way I eat. I make sure to get my share of chocolate and red wine along with fruit, veggies, nuts and grains. I eat fish, some meat and dairy and try to remember to drink water frequently. There are so many dietary theories floating around that I've concluded that moderation in all things makes the most sense.

Running fulfills my need to get outdoors every day, see what the wind and weather is up to and breathe in some outdoor air, even when it is uncomfortably hot or uncomfortably cold. I have some favorite routes. I enjoy watching as the snow covers the foothills and then as the spring run-off fills the streams. I usually run alone, starting from my doorstep, but I like being involved in a sport that keeps me in touch with a community of runners of all ages and interests. Writing about running has allowed me to get to know some amazing people and better yet, to tell their stories.

I've been lucky to travel to events, one as far away as Tokyo. It's exciting and inspiring to run in a new place, to take in the sights and sounds and to mingle with other runners who come from all over the place. At a ten-mile race in Denver, only an hour down the road from home, I paused for water at mile seven and when I glanced at my watch, was surprised to see that my time was faster than I'd anticipated. A fellow runner, a stranger, seemed to be doing the same thing. We looked at each other, smiled and took off. He stayed with me not saying much but pushing me through the last three miles to a finishing time I could never have accomplished on my own. I felt so grateful.

My family inspires me to keep on running. Three of my children have completed marathons and I have done shorter races with several of my grandchildren. One granddaughter ran her first marathon, the biggie in New York, with several cousins cheering her on. I like to think that I may have provided some incentive for my offspring to make running a permanent part of their lives. My wish and hope is that they will find the same joys that running has given me.

Showers and Sweat

When I was a ninth grader at Queen Anne High School in Seattle, Washington in 1951, the sole requirement for getting an "A" in physical education was to take 40 showers after class during the semester. I'm not kidding!

If you only managed 30 showers, you earned a "B", 20 were worth a "C" and so on. It did not matter how well you dribbled a basketball or how gracefully you touched your toes. Clever kids that we were, we soon devised a strategy that made it possible to avoid a shower and still get credit for taking one. Because the teacher did nothing more than check to make sure that the towel you turned in was wet, it wasn't too tough to dampen down a towel and turn it in.

I don't remember what kind of physical activities we engaged in during gym period, but I know for sure that there was not a single step of running in the curriculum. We would no doubt have balked at that. We were girls, after all, and girls weren't supposed to exert, heaven forbid sweat, back then, much less get out of breath.

When I moved to Philadelphia in 1952, things were different in the sports arena. The high school I attended had girls' tennis and swim teams. Girls played basketball (half-court only), field hockey and lacrosse, a funny game I'd never heard of in which you cradled a little ball in a basket on the end of a stick and you actually had to run with it. As a junior, I tried out for lacrosse and made the fourth team, the lowest of the low. I was hopeless and soon quit in disgust. Apparently there had been too many fake showers and not enough sweat in my past.

The college I attended a couple of years later was spread out across a small Ohio town—dorms up on a hill and classrooms a mile away close to downtown. Every day we walked that mile in the morning, then back to the dorm for lunch and repeated the process in the afternoon. None of us would have been caught dead on a bike, no matter how practical that would have been. Part of the problem was that we weren't allowed to attend class in pants unless the temperature was 20 degrees or lower. And besides, biking just wasn't cool.

Once I started running, I found I couldn't stop. To this day I don't feel as if I've really earned a shower unless it follows a workout that forces me to produce a little sweat.

Off and On: Struggles with Underwear

The day long ago when I paused during a run, reached inside my shirt, whipped off my bra and stuffed it in my pocket issued in a new era for me. In those days, before the advent of running bras, my straps were forever making distracting, uncomfortable trips from my shoulders and down my upper arms rendering this particular piece of underwear embarrassing and useless.

That day I began a slow decline into the ranks of those who don't wear bras at all. Now I wear one when I think I should, or—more accurately—when I think someone's going to notice that I haven't got one on. Given my druthers, I'd never wear one at all.

My history with brassieres goes back to the time I first clamped one on at age twelve. My nine-year-old brother, sensing my discomfort with this sign of approaching puberty, marched himself across the street from our house. "Libby's wearing a bra," he announced to the neighbors after he made sure I was close enough to hear. Mortified, I could feel my face turn bright red and a few unbidden tears slip down my cheeks in front of the older childless couple who had become my friends.

I have a history with underpants, too, though it is not related to running and goes back even further to when I was eight. The students at Mrs. Herrington's private school in a London suburb knew me as the new kid-- an American with a weird accent. I had a hard time understanding them so we didn't talk much.

I was small for my age and not accustomed to wearing a school uniform. I struggled with French and algebra in this new school, subjects unheard of in an American third grade and in which I was expected to "catch up."

For me, lunchtime has always ranked right up there with the worst things about being the new kid. Not having a ready-made group of friends to eat with used to bring on anxiety for me every time I moved to a new school and it happened pretty frequently.

At Mrs. Herrington's we lined up in the cafeteria to get our lunches. There I stood one day, shortly after my arrival, tray clutched in both hands, when the elastic in my Carter's cotton undies gave out and gravity took over.

Before I could squeeze my legs together to avert the inevitable, my drawers lay at my ankles for God and all those proper English children to see. I froze. I didn't drop my tray and grab for my pants. I didn't yell for help. I didn't do anything.

Amid kid giggles, the nearest teacher, a stern-looking one, disappeared and returned to hand me a piece of string. "Give me your tray," she said. "Go to the baarthroom and see what you can do." She didn't offer to help.

I disappeared and fumbled around as best I could to tie up my britches, wishing I had a safety pin. My re-entry into the cafeteria was a character-building moment in my life.

Even today I buy underwear carefully, avoiding skinny elastic. And I don't leave home without safety pins, needle and thread.

No one's going to catch me with my pants down, on the road or at lunch.

The Female Runner

Many years ago a friend of mine told me that she had quit running because her calves were getting bigger. Her decision didn't make me quit, but it did make me think. My calves have always been pretty big and if I kept on running, well, they would only get bigger— and then what?

I came across a skinny little book hidden away on my shelf called *The Female Runner*, published in 1974 by World Publications. My granddaughter Abby was visiting and we chuckled together over the foreword that begins, "The runner's world is, always has been and will for a long time to come, continue to be a man's world. Women only get to sample the leftovers from it."

It goes on to say that females make up only one percent of the running population, run in shoes designed for men, race in meets that no one notices and get what's left of expense money, prizes and publicity after the men have taken theirs.

How times have changed! These days women often outnumber men in races of all distances and garner prize money and recognition equally with men.

In less than 50 pages the book contains a whole lot of fascinating information written by males and females involved with running themselves and with training women runners in the sixties and seventies. They discuss the physical and psychological restraints that affect the performance of women runners and they advocate for change.

The ancient Greeks beheaded any female who dared to watch a warrior athlete perform. A superintendent of schools refused to let girls run cross-country because "they would just go out into the woods and get laid by the boys." Coach Kenneth Foreman was told by a colleague that he was a fool to work with female athletes because they were incapable of tolerating stress and would only get into trouble with male athletes if he let them train together.

Dr. Joan Ullyot, 3:13 marathoner and author of *Womens Running,* began running when she was 30 and has lots of experience training women runners. She commented on the irony that women were limited to running sprint events for years when their physique made them unsuitable for short explosive action and much more suited to distance events. "Women are made to run long rather than fast," she insisted. It is a proven fact that women often have better endurance than men in distance events.

During the first years that I ran, I did it with little or no thought of going faster or longer. It wasn't until I entered a race on a whim when I turned 40 that I got serious about improving my running. The marathon distance seemed so impossible that I decided to try training for one. Finishing my first marathon made me feel powerful and fueled my determination to keep on running.

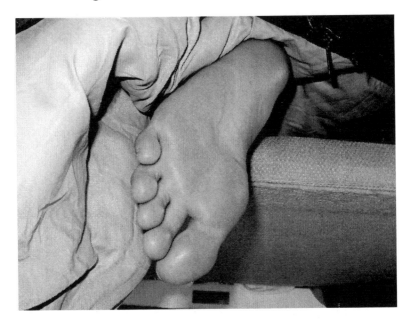

Getting Out the Door

There's something called the "annoyance barrier" that has the power to keep you from going out for a run, especially when the wind is whistling, the rain is pounding down or the temperature has dipped well below comfortable or above tolerable. The barrier could show up as something as innocent as a question from someone close to you in a warm bed that mumbles, "You're not going out in this weather, are you?" Perhaps you say to yourself, *I'll wait until this afternoon. It will be warmer then.* Or, *I'll go in the evening, when it is cooler.* Risky decision. Life is way too likely to intrude and mess up your plan.

Perhaps by now you are over the hump. That is, you've been running long enough to know that you are definitely going to get in some miles on this day; you may not be excited about braving the wind, but you'll go because you *need* to go, you *want* to go, no matter how miserable you know the first mile will be. Before long, you'll warm up, the kinks in the knees will loosen and the familiar little aches and pains will diminish. Sometimes, to your surprise, you'll slip into "the zone" and have a great run despite— maybe even because of--the weather.

No.? Don't buy it? Okay. Maybe it won't happen like that every time you brave the elements, but most people who run regularly will tell you that no matter how hard it may be to get out the door, they are never sorry that they went. Below are some gimmicks designed to pry you out of bed, into your running clothes, layer after layer if need be, and out into cold, darkness, wind, and even snow.

Make a date with a friend. Commit to showing up at a specified time and place. You'll be less likely to cancel when someone is counting on you. A couple of my friends have been meeting at 6 a.m. Monday, Wednesday and Friday mornings, regardless of temperature and conditions, for long enough that it has become a sacred routine.

Plan ahead. Decide what you're going to wear and lay out your clothes the night before. Sounds silly, but it represents a tiny bit of commitment that can be helpful.

Remind yourself that a run is necessary, that it will give you energy and allow you to bring added enthusiasm to whatever task you undertake that day. There's no better time or place to problem solve than on a run. I've often wished that some smart person would invent a convenient mechanism, maybe to hang around your neck, for preserving the ideas that pop into my head while out on the road. If you take a smart phone along and can juggle it easily, perhaps it can serve this purpose. But for me, that is weight and worry that I do not need.

If you're new enough to running that it hasn't yet become second nature, try this; use the mantra of a cross country coach and runner with an infectious sense of humor. "Start slow and taper off," he'll tell you with a twinkle in his eye. Be easy on yourself as you get started in this running game.

Measure out a one-mile course beginning at your own front door if that is possible. Decide how many days of the week you are going to run and insert them into your calendar. Three is a good number to start with. Then go out and conquer that one-mile course. Start slowly. When you run out of gas, stop and walk. Once you've caught your breath and are smiling again, begin a comfortable jog.

Repeat this scenario until you've made it to the end of the mile. When you can run the whole mile without stopping to walk, you're ready to add some distance; but no more than five minutes more per run or a total of five miles more in any given week.

And keep a smile on your face, even when it hurts. That means you are having fun.

The scene at the finish

Boston Marathon 1980

In a letter I wrote to Boston Marathon Race Director Will Cloney in 1979 after I had completed my second Denver Marathon in three hours, 29 minutes and 47 seconds, I asked if my time was good enough to qualify for his race in 1980.

The fact that he answered me was a surprise. After all, I didn't even know his name so I addressed my letter to Race Director, Boston Marathon. I knew the qualifying time for all women had been lowered to three hours and 20 minutes for

1980. I didn't think it fair that there was no qualifying time for masters women (over 40) as there was for men.

I was testing him. I assumed that organizing the marathon was a huge task and I guessed that much of the personal touch had gone out of it. With faint hope for a reply, I wrote the letter anyway.

I received a kind note stating that if my time had been run in a certified race, he would allow me to enter officially. I was surprised. He told me to mail in my application with the $5 non-refundable entry fee.

The following months were filled with thoughts like *should I do this?* a couple of infuriating colds, and a Colorado winter of record-breaking snowfalls making training difficult. There was lots of urging from my family about this "once in a lifetime" opportunity that swayed me. On April 19, I boarded a plane on my way to Boston. My nervousness lessened once I realized that now there was no way out.

When a most unfortunate fellow in the seat in front of me, also on his way to run the marathon, swallowed the pull-tab from a beer can somewhere over Kansas, things fell into perspective. Running the Boston Marathon was important and scary, but it was not a matter of life and death. The fellow sat quietly until we arrived in Boston where an ambulance was waiting for him.

Seeing my name and number, **W430** out of 449 women entered in the race, in the *Boston*

Globe was exciting. There were 4945 men entered. The media paid lots of attention to this race. At the time, races of any distance in Colorado and the surrounding states went virtually unnoticed in the press.

My brother and sister-in-law gave me a ride from their home in New Hampshire to the start. The place was a carnival. Hawkers were offering T-shirts and programs with a history of the race. Kids were selling Kool-Aid, and the good women of Hopkinton were selling homemade baked goods. No one who lived in Hopkinton could get out of town that day except on foot, but it seemed no one wanted to miss any of the excitement.

At 11:20 a.m. the runners began a slow movement from Hopkinton High School toward the start about a half-mile away on the main street of town. Near the end of the gathered runners, in a section of their own, women with numbers between 211 and 449 and men over 40 with numbers over 5000 lined up.

Behind this last group of official runners (those with numbers) hordes of unofficial runners assembled. Among them a fellow with a sign that read "back of the pack" offered fake numbers for $1.

A kind woman shared her water bottle with me, a couple of runners made a last minute dash to the facilities, another smeared Vaseline on some critical spots and left the jar on the curb. A cannon boomed and we were off—at least those ahead of us were. Those of us toward the back began walking making wisecracks about the comfortable pace.

By the end of the first mile, heat became an issue. It radiated up from the pavement, intensified by the thousands of feet passing over it. I made a decision to drink as much as I could and accept a dousing from a cooling hose whenever my shirt dried out. Others steered clear of the water, even shouting at people to stop spraying them.

I was thrilled to spot the venerable John Kelley running in his 49th Boston Marathon, thriving on the cheers and outstretched hands of the crowd. In his long career, he had won the race twice and would continue to run it until 1992. He died at the age of 97 in 2004.

I saw a blind runner with a sign on his back indicating he could not see, running independently and at a good pace, guided by the words and occasional touch of his friend. Twin women dressed alike ran by me, sticking together as the crowd urged them on.

Time passed. Every few miles there were tables with cups of water and an electrolyte drink. Running past these tables was like running through a paper cup carpet, crunching and kicking cups out of the way as we ran by. There were official Boston Athletic Association aid stations every five miles but in between, spectators offered orange and grapefruit slices, hard candy, water-soaked sponges, damp rags and facial tissues. Children held out their hands, hoping runners would high five them as they went by. A father had his son calling out numbers of names listed in the newspaper and then shouted out, "Go, John" or "Go Joe" as the runners passed by.

The women of Wellesley College had become famous for their enthusiasm. They crowded so close to the center of the road that only two runners abreast could pass by. They shouted and cheered, offering special encouragement to the women. When I realized that runners had been pouring past these women for an hour and a half by the time I arrived, their enthusiasm became even more remarkable.

From one small New England town to another, 5,394 of us were wending our way toward Boston and the finish line. At mile 17 the hills became a welcome diversion for some who needed a break from the monotony of the flat course. A Fort Collins friend living in Boston called out my name and gave me a psychological lift I needed. Then it was back to work on Heartbreak Hill which really doesn't compare to the ups and downs I'm used to in the foothills close to home. Still, it came at a point when my energy was low and did present a challenge. I slowed and shortened my steps and soon the ups were behind me and it was all down hill into Boston.

I glanced at the skyline. I felt a small sea breeze. Big white numerals on the road said 24. *Is it possible to go another 2.2 miles?* I asked myself. "Almost there," came a shout from the crowd of onlookers. "The worst is over."

"Like hell," I said to the nearest runner. "A mile to go," another spectator called out. None of us knew for certain how much farther we had to go. Then a fellow held up a sign that read, " .6 TO GO. ACCURATE."

And then it was over. An overhead digital time blinked away the seconds letting each runner know his exact finishing time. Then down the chutes we went, into a parking garage where heat reflecting blankets, yogurt and granola bars were offered. All I wanted was water.

Bill Rodgers set the course record that year with a time of 2:09:27. Rosie Ruiz was declared the female winner until it was discovered that she had hopped a subway for part of the course. Jacqueline Gareau, with a time of 2:34:28, was not officially declared winner until the following day.

The laurel wreaths had been placed on winning brows hours ago, but still the runners streamed in, looking a little glassy-eyed, some more destroyed by the heat and the distance than others. Soon there were bodies sitting and lying all over the plaza. A few runners ended up in the medical tent having fluid pumped into bodies that, because of heat exhaustion, wouldn't accept it any other way. It was 8 p.m. before the last runner arrived Only his daughter waited for him in the darkness.

There were few personal bests on this day when the temperature rose to 80 degrees.

But there was plenty of personal satisfaction for everyone who finished the 84th running of the most famous marathon of them all with the possible exception of the original course in Greece.

They dispersed quickly, these runners from 42 countries and every state in the U.S., fading into the anonymity of the bustling city. Here and there, the next day, I spotted someone walking stiff-legged and climbing steps gingerly and felt an instant bond.

I was full of gratitude for the kindness of Will Cloney. The following year, as he entered his fourth decade as race director, a three hour 30 minute qualifying time was instituted for masters women runners. I felt proud to have had something to do with that. The race continued to grow, but Will never got a pay raise for his work. It remained what it had always been—nothing. He died in 2003 at age 91. I was sorry that I never met him.

Jacqueline Gareau with Libby James, 2018

Staying warm

The Battle in Seattle

Colorado sun welcomed me home from the
"Battle in Seattle." I suffered no war wounds.
In fact, I wasn't even sore. I was just happy to
be back in the sunshine after my first cross-
country running experience.

With a Boulder Road Runners team, I
competed in the United States Track and

Field Association National Club Championships on December 10, 2011. In the masters division, more than 150 women over 40, from all across the country, attacked a 6k distance on the slick, damp grass of a golf course.

Seattle-classic cloud cover and a forty-degree temperature reading called for an extra layer of clothing plus gloves and headband for me. Spirits ran high as the masters men and women competed first, followed by the young folks; men's and women's open divisions (under age 40).

At 5 p.m. it was standing room only in the ballroom at the Seattle Renaissance Hotel where awards were presented. Individual and team winners received rowdy cheers, applause and medals for their accomplishments. A celebratory dinner completed a memorable evening. The "age-graded" award I was given took me by surprise. I had never heard of such a thing, calculated by combining one's age and time in a formula I still do not understand. But I liked it!

There's a camaraderie among those committed to most any sport that makes one thankful for the existence of the human community. Running is no exception. It took a huge number of dedicated people to pull off the USATF event at such a professional level. The last minute details were tended to in damp, nasty conditions. Volunteers along the course shouted encouragement to runners all day long.

I jumped at the opportunity to go to Seattle, because I had never run on a team or in a cross-country meet, but also because I have connections there. My grandson Adam, newly-graduated from college, had recently moved to Seattle. I crashed on his couch for a few nights. During my stay, I came to appreciate the graceful way he and his two roommates approached jobs, graduate school, keeping house, and living harmoniously together. In their neighborhood, we ate pizza at Tutti Bella, and saw *A Child's Christmas in Wales* at Stone Soup Theatre. We hung out for a while at an Ultimate Frisbee tournament where Adam and his girlfriend, Allison, played with youthful enthusiasm.

I once in lived in Seattle, and after nearly fifty years, I'm still in touch with long-time friends from my days at Queen Anne High School. I was in town long enough to catch up with their lives and reminisce over a long lazy lunch overlooking Puget Sound. Saturday evening the generations came together as another of my high school friends and her husband entertained Allison, Adam, and me for a festive beef bourguignon dinner. What does all this this rambling have to do with running? I'd like to suggest that should an opportunity arise to participate in a running event in a place where you have a history, or that you're curious about, or where you have special friends--GO! Don't talk yourself out of it because you don't have time, it's too expensive, or it's a whole lot of trouble to pack up and travel. The memories you come away with will far outweigh any possible downsides.

Wherever I go, I'm always grateful to be home again. This time I was more than usually appreciative of the Colorado sunshine.

Still Running

Pam Iyer

From Sea to Shining Sea

This land is my land, this land is your land from the redwood forest, to the gulfstream waters, this land was made for running free. Pam Iyer of Fort Collins didn't sing this modified verse to me when we talked, but I left with the tune in my head. That and *fifty nifty United States...from 13 original colonies...*

Between January 2009 and June 2011, Iyer, then 56, raced a half marathon in every single state, beginning in Carlsbad, California and ending in Kona, Hawaii. She ran through cacti, along sea coasts, on an island, in redwood forests, in a cypress swamp, in vineyards, on horse trails, through Amish country, over covered bridges, to Hoover Dam, around Crazy Horse Monument, past banks of snow so high she couldn't see the ocean from the coast road course, past many state capitols, and once finished a race on the fifty-yard line in the Rose Bowl Stadium.

Forty-two times she won her age group, 55-59 or 50-59 in smaller races. In the Dismal Swamp race in Florida she won a hand-carved bird on a tall stand that she could hardly get home, a dog tag with her name imprinted on it in a Memorial Day race in Lenox, Massachusetts, a hot wheels VW bus in Michigan, and a piece of rock from Crazy Horse Monument in South Dakota. She ate chocolate at every aid station at the Mud and Chocolate Race, was handed a flashlight to get through a mile-long tunnel in Wisconsin, zigzagged in and out of cacti and clambered up enormous boulders in Arizona, sloshed through a downpour in Connecticut, and baked in 95-degee heat as she climbed endless steps in the Double Dipsea in California.

At the time, Pam worked in the office at Rivendell, a private school in Fort Collins and except during the summer months, had to squeeze her races into weekends. She learned so much about finding cheap airfares that she began to feel qualified to be a travel agent. She found a $98 round-trip Denver to Oklahoma and another time drove to California so she could fly from Los Angeles to Hawaii rather than taking the expensive flight from Denver.

Fond memories for Pam are running the Colorado Half Marathon in her hometown with her daughter Kristin who was doing her first, and completing a race in Napa Valley with Rachel Pettit, an 11-year-old student at Rivendell School.

Her fastest half marathon was an hour and 37 minutes in Deadwood, South Dakota. Her slowest time is difficult to compute since several of her races were 25k trail runs, longer than the 13.1 mile half-marathon distance. But she doesn't care much about times. What she loved most was visiting different parts of the country, getting to know the people and the culture, and using the little free time she had to see the local sights.

In Alaska, the half-marathon started in downtown Anchorage close to the J. C. Penney's store. Racers were warned to beware of moose once they got out of town. She ran with 8,000 others on the coast in Long Branch, New Jersey and with several dozen runners in Iowa—destination a town called Marathon. When Frank Shorter presented Pam with her award in Kona, Hawaii, he learned she was from Colorado, his home state, and promptly kissed her on the cheek.

In 2012, when I spoke with her, Pam indicated that she just might do the whole 50-state routine all over again. By June of 2014 she was busy making travel plans for the coming fall. She had continued to do a half marathon *somewhere* at least once a month, sometimes more often.

Four years later she found herself only four states short of running a half-marathon in every state in the union not twice, not three, but FOUR times, with the exception of Alaska, Hawaii, South Carolina and New Hampshire. Now retired from her job, she has much more flexibility with her travels.

She's usually at home during the week where she's a regular at her health club. "I'm working on defeating this aging thing," she said. "I roll out of bed early and hit the health club whether I feel like it or not." Because she does a long run most weekends, she limits her mileage during the week.

Pam makes sure that every race she enters is one that is new to her "I choose unique races in places I've never been to before," she said. "I like to experience cultures that are different from my own. I've learned from my travels that there are many ways to get something done and no one way is the only right way."

In January 2018 she travelled to Death Valley in California and to Orlando and St. Petersburg in Florida for races. In March she returned to California to visit a friend and to run a half-marathon. She also plans a race combined with a visit to her sister in Houston, Texas in 2018.

Pam has not limited herself to racing across the United States. With a nephew, she did a half-marathon on the summer solstice above the Arctic Circle in Iceland. The race started in bright daylight at 10:30 p.m. and it was still light when the race finished hours later. The king and queen of Norway came to shoot the gun to start the race. In September 2017 she journeyed to France and Italy to spend time with her youngest son who was living in France. While there she ran a half-marathon on the Tour de France course.

These days she knows so much about economy travel and lodging that friends come to her for advice. They hope one day she will share her experiences with them in written form. She's thinking about it as she continues on a unique life journey.

Libby James

Felix Wong

It All Began with a Five-dollar Bike

In 2010 Felix Wong ran the Davy Crockett
Marathon in Crockett, Texas, on a Saturday.
His time of 3 hours and 12 minutes was good
enough for first place. The next day he ran
another 26.2 miles in the Big D Marathon in
Dallas, Texas in 4 hours and 40 minutes—not
good enough to win. But he had such a good
time that in September 2012, he decided to
do another back-to-back marathon weekend.

"I hadn't done a marathon in 18 months
and I hadn't averaged more than 30 miles of
training a week, but here was an opportunity
too good to pass up," Wong said. He'd been
working on running a marathon in all 50
states and here were two, in two different
states, on two consecutive days. He finished
18th overall in Bismarck, North Dakota, then

jumped into his car and drove to Billings, Montana to compete in the Montana Marathon the following day.

He drove alone, immersing himself in the study of Mandarin on a CD, and enjoying the great scenery. "No distractions," he said. "I was brushing up on my French so I spent some time on it as well." He'd planned to camp out on his trip but work deadlines forced him into more traditional lodging.

Who is this guy, and what makes him tick? Born of parents who grew up in China and emigrated to Canada before moving to the U.S. Felix is the second of three brothers raised in rural southern California. As a kid, his world opened up when he bought a bike for $5 at a garage sale and discovered the freedom to go. He borrowed a "better bike" to do his first century ride as a senior in high school, an experience that made him more than a little saddle sore and at the same time cemented a lifetime commitment to long distance exercise.

A degree in mechanical engineering from Stanford led to a position in the semiconductor industry, and in 2005, relocation to Fort Collins, Colorado where he consults and has time to indulge his love of outdoor sports and travel. He chose his new home carefully, researching scores of towns in 19 states and Canada until he found the one that matched up with his list of qualifications. He has never regretted the time and effort he invested in choosing Fort Collins as his home. He returns to California several times a year to see family and meet with a major client.

The hardest thing he's ever done? The Tour Divide bicycle ride from Canada to Mexico, 2,700 miles in 27 days including encounters with wipeouts, wrong turns, and starvation. At one point he found himself so desperate for food that he flagged down a car. The Pepsi and half a hamburger he was given lasted him until another traveler took him home for dinner. The following day he subsisted on tortillas, soup and peanuts before he found a town with a grocery store. "I learned to be better prepared," he said.

Wong is happiest when he has a very long way to go. He has competed three of Colorado's most challenging double century (200-mile) cycling events known as the Triple Crown. He also breezed through the 607-mile Camino de Santiago in Spain on his feet in 20.4 days. Figure out *that* daily mileage!

He has completed three-dozen marathons, two 100-mile runs and countless shorter runs and long distance bike rides. In 2015, Wong earned eighth place in the Trans America Bike Race. By 2017 he had added more stunning accomplishments to his resume, including completing marathons in 33 states. Because of his cross-country biking experience, Wong is looking forward to acting as crew chief for See to See, a team of eight cyclists on tandems, four sighted and four blind, as they pedal 3,100 miles in the

Race Across America in the summer of 2018. Cut-off time for the event is nine days.

When the race is over, Wong will be busy doing a double century bike ride and adding another state to his marathon total. Perhaps all that activity will adequately prepare him to ride his 41-pound, one-speed Huffy bicycle from his doorstep in Fort Collins to the little mountain town of Walden and back home again, exactly a 200-mile round trip. "Gotta do it," he promises. "It is the only one of my six bicycles that hasn't made the trip."

36,000 competed in the Tokyo Marathon

Lost in the Land of the Rising Sun

Every decade or so, one of my kids talks me into doing a marathon. This time it was Kurt, my son who at the time headed up McDonald's Hamburgers supply chain for Japan in Tokyo. There were multiple reasons for running a marathon in Tokyo. It was a chance to be with grandchildren that I see rarely, travel with my Wyoming daughter and son-in-law, and celebrate my friend Cathy Morgan's 65th birthday and first-ever marathon.

We packed a whole lot into six days, travelling by train, foot, taxi, and subway. We admired the Meiji shrine in Yoyogi Park, Tokyo's answer to Central Park in New York. We cruised around the world's largest fish market in the early-morning rain, and afterwards appreciated the welcoming warmth and expansive breakfast buffet at the luxurious American Club.

We shared little plates of exotic fish and veggies at a restaurant where each diner squeezes a fresh grapefruit and concocts a delicious drink, not for himself, but for the person sitting next to him at the table. "Eating is much more social here," Kurt explained as he ordered for us all. "It's not like in the states where you order your own dinner and eat it all yourself." The highlight of that evening was a magic show in a setting so intimate that a total stranger in the small audience, learning it was Cathy's birthday, ran out to the street and bought her a beautiful bouquet of roses.

Sunday morning it was down to business. For the first time ever, I rode a taxi to a race start. There were so many people that it took 30 minutes to drop a clothes bag and find my assigned spot in the line-up of 36,000 people, packed so closely together that the cold was no longer an issue. Twenty minutes after booming fireworks announced the start, I finally crossed the starting line. The course, flat with a little downhill, ran through the city with two long out-and-back sections. When I reached the 20-mile mark where I'd promised myself a walk if needed, I kept on running, anxious for the last miles to be behind me. Crowds of spectators along the way offered dried plums, candies, and at one point even beer or wine. Thousands of volunteers saw to it that there was plenty of water, electrolyte drink, medical assistance, and encouragement.

The first 26 miles were manageable. It was the next two, or was it as many as three miles, that became a challenge. After a subdued finish where spectators were barred and there was no hoopla to welcome the runners, I began to walk, following the orderly stream of human traffic that flowed, up, down, and around the Tokyo Big Site conference center. Before long I'd completely lost my bearings.

The day before, while picking up race packets at the conference center, we'd spotted a small McDonald's restaurant where we planned to meet. Fifty McDonald's employees ran in the race, and hundreds more cheered us on as we passed by in our yellow McDonald's *Smile Runner* shirts. It seemed an appropriate place to gather. But after the race, obscured by milling crowds, and hobbled by no knowledge of the language and the lack of a cell phone, it took me 90 minutes to find our meeting place.

Never, in all my life, had I been so happy to see the golden arches.

A gentle touch and a few soft words

Don't Go in the Road

Early on this morning as I ran west toward
the foothills without a single car in sight, I
came across a man and his dog. I was running
facing traffic in the bike lane, bordered on the
right by a very visible, newly-painted white
line. The man, his dog and I were going in the
same direction. As I approached from behind,
the dog stepped over the white line into the
traffic lane. The man stopped.

Instead of yanking on his dog's leash, this
man quietly told his dog to sit, which the dog
did, looking a little dolefully at his owner.
Instead of yelling at his dog, which part of me
expected this man to do, he got down on his
knees and stroked the dog's head. Then he

looked into the dog's eyes and said simply, "Don't go in the road."

Now, I'm not sure if this dog, or any dog, understands when it comes to white lines on the road. But after watching this man and his dog, I suspect that there are some dogs, if properly taught, who can learn to beware of the white line on the road and respect it as a boundary, They may not ever know why but will comply because they wish to please their master. Maybe they will even come to trust that the boundary is there for their own good. That somehow it exists to keep them safe.

White lines, in one form or another, are all about. They keep us on the straight and narrow, urge us to do what is right, for our own good, to keep us safe, to make sure we take our turn, to keep us "in line."

Sometimes we humans balk. There are lines we disagree with. We're in a hurry or we just don't give a hoot and we step over. But most of us, most of the time, take note of the white line and stay inside it. We know it is there for a reason.

It's a rocky road out there. As I continued on my run, I got to thinking that we'd all be better off if we did a little less yelling and yanking. Instead we might offer a gentle touch and a few words spoken softly—to our dogs and to each other.

There's no avoiding the road. We have to head on out there but it wouldn't hurt to be aware of the white line and hug our dogs.

Post Marathon Strategies

So. You've been thinking about doing a marathon for quite a while? You've made the decision to go for it. There are hundreds of marathons around to choose from. It's a good idea to pick one as close as possible to home to keep things as simple and easy as possible.

Now you're all signed up, entry fee paid. You know when it is, and where it is, and you've found yourself a training schedule. You're out there on the roads, putting in the miles you need to run before the big day arrives.

The moment will come, yes, I promise, *it will*, when the race is over. And for a little while, before post-race euphoria sets in, it's likely you won't feel so good. In fact, during those moments, you may swear that you'll *never do this again.* But before you know it, you'll be one happy camper, basking in your accomplishment and deciding that if you can run 26.2 miles, well, you are pretty close to invincible.

For the next couple of days, you may find yourself stiff enough to descend stairs backwards and groan when you get up out of a chair or off the ground. Then the day will come when you feel anxious to hit the road again. There are all kinds of advice out there on post-marathon recovery. Here are some guidelines you might want to consider:

1. Some say recovering from a marathon takes one or two weeks. Others claim a person should consider himself "injured" for 26 days, a day for each mile of the race. The duration of recovery depends upon a person's fitness level and the intensity of effort put forth. Only you can decide when you feel ready to begin running again. There's no point in rushing it.

2. Before the race, try to stick closely to your training schedule. A session or two skipped won't matter much, especially if it is within the last couple of weeks before the race, but be conscientious about getting in your mileage. Stay faithful to your weekly long run. It is especially important and will pay off on race day by preparing you psychologically to go farther when it counts. The more it hurts before the race, the less it will hurt afterwards.

3. Be diligent about pacing yourself during the race. It is easy to go out too fast but you'll be sorry if you do and are forced to do the last few miles in "survival mode." Worse yet, you may end up with some issues that even a week in a hot tub won't cure.

4. Drink at every opportunity. I can't emphasize this enough. A couple of sips will do nicely. Stick to water unless you have trained using an

energy drink and know it won't upset your stomach.

5. After the race, get off your feet as soon as possible and have something to drink. Soft drinks are good because of their high sugar content. Get some food into your body in the first 30 minutes after the race when it will be absorbed most readily.

6. Be mellow about your running for as long as several weeks. Now is the perfect time to enjoy walking, biking or swimming—activities that are fun and use different muscle groups.

7. Listen to your body. Everyone is different. Don't go back to hard training until you find yourself eager to do so.

8. Give yourself a pat on the back for a job well done.

Remembering Cathy

The Wild West Relay

The brainchild of Paul Vanderheiden, Wild West Relay, aptly subtitled *Get Your Ass Over the Pass,* is a 200-mile team event held each year during the first part of August when the moon is closest to full. It first took place in 2005 and for many runners it has become a zany tradition over the years. Piling into a van with five other bodies for an overnight adventure through the foothills and deep into the Rocky Mountains of Colorado, into three national forests and over two passes may not sound like everyone's cup of tea. But believe me, it grows on you and you keep coming back for more.

Here's how it works: The run is divided into 36 segments, distances between three and nine miles. Most teams consist of 12 runners but some hardy souls form teams of six. The twelve-member teams are divided equally into two vans, one "active" and the other "inactive" during the event. When the runners in van one have completed their assigned run segment, van two takes over and the runners in van one have five or six hours to rest before they become active again.

I've done the relay several times but the years that stand out for me are 2012 when I was part of an all-woman team and 2017 when I ran with a team that had a special purpose in mind.

In 2012, the first runner on our team started at 5:40 a.m. on Friday morning August 3, from Budweiser Brewery north of Fort Collins, Colorado. The route headed north toward the rural community of Livermore, site of the first changeover stop where the last of van one's six runners finished their leg and tagged off to the first runner from van two.

It was mid-morning by the time volunteers at the Livermore Community Center welcomed runners with food, drinks and a place to rest. Each of the stops is manned by volunteers, and all proceeds from the food

Libby James

and drink they offer go to a non-profit organization of their choosing. Also, the race pays for their help, using part of the registration fee for the race. This money also goes to charities.

Our all-female team--two 50-somethings, four bouncing teens, two grandmas, an educator, an exercise physiologist, an attorney, and a hairdresser—we were all in this together. One of us had been training for a marathon, another hadn't trained at all and the rest had at least made some sort of effort to prepare for the three laps each had been assigned. The teens hadn't trained much but they were game, young and tough. They slept easily in the van and laughed, joked and played loud music to entertain themselves.

Around midnight our van pulled into the tiny mountain town of Walden. It was our turn to become "inactive," which meant that we had about six hours to sleep. I rolled out my sleeping bag on the damp grass of the high school football field. By the time I crawled into it my feet were so cold that I knew sleep would not come easily. I lay there and relived my first run in the hot sun of midday, and my second, in the cool dark of the night. If my head weren't so small, maybe my headlamp would have stayed in place on my forehead and I wouldn't have had to wear it around my shoulder. Bobbing up and down as it did, it didn't offer much focused light. Thank goodness for a nearly full moon. A tall male speedster flew by as I approached the last mile of my segment, but slowed enough

51

to ask if I'd seen the falling star. "A really good one," he assured me.

"Missed it," I mumbled, sorry that I'd been looking down at my feet instead of up into the sky.

As first light dawned in Walden, the sprinklers came to life on the football field and I was suddenly wide awake. There was no time to worry about a soggy sleeping bag as it was time to be on the road again.

As the members of our team plodded their way one at a time up and over Rabbit Ears Pass and down the other side on Saturday, the temperature rose steadily nearing 90 degrees by the time we reached the outskirts of Steamboat Springs. Abby, our last runner, my 18-year-old granddaughter, was plugging along the bike path at the edge of town toward the finish line. The other eleven members of our team were waiting near the finish to join her so that we could all cross the line together. I was tired, my quads were screaming, but I decided to head down the bike path, meet up with Abby and run to the finish with her. Red-faced, she was breathing so hard that she could hardly speak. She whispered, "This is the hardest thing I've ever done." And a few minutes later nearly out of breath, "Thanks for coming to meet me."

I choked up. Ridiculous. Yet, that moment was, for me, the high point of a trip that can't really be described.

In August of 2017, I signed up to do Wild West again on a team with the unlikely name of HumpalOtt for Morgan. Some weekends fly by with nothing special to remember them by. But not this past weekend for the 500 or so Wild West Relay runners who made their way, some for the first time, others for the twelfth, 200 miles from Fort Collins through Colorado's Rocky Mountains, into Wyoming and back to Colorado for the finish. We started early on Friday morning, August 4, and finished on Saturday afternoon in Gondola Square in Steamboat Springs.

The route was the same as in past years, through the towns Livermore and Red Feather Lakes, over Deadmans Pass into Woods Landing, Wyoming and back into Walden, Colorado before ascending Rabbit Ears Pass and descending into Steamboat Springs. Members of the 61 teams who participated were there to have a good time. I'd run with this team in the past, and I was glad to be back to repeat the experience with them.

Every year we confronted the same logistical challenges—finding a couple of suitable vans, planning food and lodging, and training enough so that we can approach our assigned distances with a reasonable hope of contributing to the team effort. We were in a "helter-skelter" category which meant we weren't taking this thing too seriously and we weren't after any spectacular finishing time. We knew this was an adventure run more than a race, making fun and camaraderie way more important than competing with oneself or anyone else.

Local Realtor John Humpal and physical therapist Brad Ott organized this team several years ago, and both of them were quite pleased with the creativity and humor of the team's name. This year the team was running in honor of one of our loyal, long-time team members who died way too young last January—thus the addition of her name making our team this year HumpalOtt for Morgan. We carried photos of Cathy Morgan in our vans, had special shirts emblazoned with a photo of her smiling as she ran. As we cruised up and down the hills, we thought of her and told story after Morgan story, remembering a truly unforgettable person. "She's still with us, making sure we have a good time," one member of the team said. And she was. The event became a positive experience for all of us. It took some of the sting out of losing her. It made us feel better. And when all 12 of us gathered at the finish line wearing our lime green "Morgan" shirts to complete the last steps together, it was cause for celebration.

We hung around Steamboat Springs for dinner together on Saturday night and for breakfast the following morning before going our separate ways with a whole new set of memories and the hope that next year we'll do it again. For the record: we came in fourteenth in the Helter Skelter division with a total time of 33 hours, 25 minutes, 53 seconds. Our pace was 10:08-minute miles. We were not dead last.

In front of limousine, Denver bound

Thanks for Having Me

The above is a phrase that has been in my head for a long time, begging for a story to accompany it. As a National Public Radio addict, I hear it again and again when guests are interviewed. No matter who they are, almost without exception, when they have finished speaking they respond to their interviewer with those few simple words. On April 19, 2012 those words took on a whole new meaning for me.

I had such a good time when I was inducted into the Colorado Running Hall of Fame that I wanted to thank everyone...The Hall of Fame for having me...Alan Lind, an old friend, who I know had a role in making this happen...the people who interviewed me...those who sent cards and gifts...my children and grandchildren who gathered from all over...my cousins who came from the UK...and my feet for holding on long enough for me to receive this incredible honor.

It didn't start out as a very big deal. At least I didn't think so... On a Wednesday afternoon in February, I got a phone call from Maureen Roben, whom I remembered as an outstanding runner from the days when I did the Denver Marathon. She asked if I would like to be inducted into the hall of fame. That was an easy question to answer.

Little did I know how this thing would mushroom. My daughters started making decisions. They assured me that my sons, who lived in Florida and Tokyo would come. They planned a party. My brother suggested we all ride to Denver in a limo, an idea that I thought silly at first but that ended up agreeing was brilliant.

I asked my daughters to introduce me at the ceremony, then got concerned when I learned that my sons were coming. They worked it out together electing Kristin, the oldest to speak. Jeni, the youngest, stood by her side and sons Kurt and Jeff came to the podium to meet me when I was finished with my five-minute talk.

I spoke about "aid stations," not water and Gatorade, but all the people who have supported me in my running. Hearing the stories of the other inductees was a fascinating journey into the Colorado running community. I felt so honored to be a part of this group of dedicated, talented runners.

Every card and note I received went into a little book so that I can remember the details of this occasion. A few weeks later I helped with a race organized by a 15-year-old high school student to fulfill requirements for her International Baccalaureate personal project. Proceeds went to the local food bank. I wouldn't have been so eager to volunteer if I hadn't been so grateful for what the running community has done for me.

I intend to keep on running for as long as I can with a new awareness of the importance of giving, my way of saying *thanks for having me.*

Below are the words of my talk.

I'm glad that I took up running in later life. Chances are, if I'd run in high school or college, and if I'd been any good at it at all, I'd have quit long ago—burned out or disgusted with my progressively slower times.

As it is, I didn't run at all until I was 35, and I didn't run a race until I was 40—over the hill. I did okay in my age group, partly because there weren't very many female runners in their 40s in the 1970s. Nothing like a little success to keep you at something!

By the time I entered my 70s, some of the competition had melted away, and here I am enjoying being an old lady runner! Running has taught me to keep on keeping on, even when it didn't seem worthwhile. It has allowed me to set some sort of an example by doing rather than telling, for kids and grandkids. There are three grandkids who can for sure outrun me now—and very soon there will be more.

Running has given me the opportunity to travel—this year (2012) to Seattle, Tokyo and New York for races, and to enjoy all the fun that goes along with that. Another story for another time.

Running has been the connecting link for lots of friendships and random interactions with people that I would not have met otherwise. A year ago in September I was running in Park to Park, a 10-mile race through four of Denver's parks. It is a beautiful course and it was a beautiful day. The course is a gentle downhill for a good part of it. I knew about the time I thought I could run it in, and every so often I checked my watch to see how I was doing. When I got to mile seven I paused for a drink of water and was surprised to see that I was ahead of schedule. A guy beside me looked at his watch and must have had the same thought. We looked at each other, and said, "Hey. Let's *GO!*

For the last three miles of the Park to Park, this miscellaneous man, who I later learned was in his late 50's, paced me. He stayed at my side or a little ahead, and made sure I kept up with him. I knew he could have gone faster, but for whatever reasons, he had decided that he was going to get me to run the best race I could. We didn't have the breath to talk much, but I do remember him saying, "Well, I hadn't planned to work this hard today."

He finished seven seconds ahead of me. My time was 1:19:22 which turned out to be good enough for a world's best in my 75-79 age group. I was three minutes faster than a woman in the UK who set the record in 2008.

When I caught my breath, I asked my pacer who he was and where he was from. His name is, no, not John, but Bill Doe, and I learned he was from Fort Collins! A few minutes later, he introduced me to his wife, Sue, an English professor at Colorado State University who had also run the race. Instant friends.

I run for lots of reasons—I love to be outdoors, I can eat with abandon, and I'm energized by the challenge, but when I think back over the last 40 years on the road, it has to be the people that make the memories, that have been my "Aid Stations" along the way. I'd like to tell you about a few of them:

My family has been forever supportive. My husband did not run, but often came to races with me. The day after he died in 1991. My brother John called and asked if I wouldn't like to go for a run. My brother David hauled me from his home in Nashua, NH to the start of the Boston Marathon and home again in 1980. That was an all-day undertaking.

The 2000 Steamboat Marathon, which I did with my daughters, Kristin and Jeni, was a peak experience for me. And then there is Kurt, who conned me into going to Tokyo by promising a plane ticket if I'd run the 2012 marathon with him. What could I say? Jeff is not a runner, but happily endures all the running stuff and cheers us on. And then there are my two sons-in-law who are such nice guys. They've put up with me staying in their homes so many times over the years, and are always willing to run with me.

There's "fresh legs" Cathy Morgan who came to the game late in life and completed her first marathon in Tokyo, three days after her 65th birthday. She was one who NEVER said no to an adventure.

I figured I'd have a good Bolder Boulder run when, standing in line to use the porta potty before the race, a door opened, and out stepped Frank Shorter. Then it was my turn and I got to use that specially anointed porta potty. So, thanks to Frank.

At mile 18 of the Steamboat Marathon in 2000 a fellow runner said, "Can I ask you a question?"

"Sure," I answered. "Would it by any chance be age-related?"

"Yes." He said. "How old are you?"

"Sixty-three," I answered. And then we visited and I learned about several of his marathons and of his favorite course, the Ocean-to-Ocean along the coast of South Africa adjacent to the Atlantic and Indian Oceans. He made the miles fly by.

I chatted with Trip Applequist, a rancher from Farson, Wyoming on the way to the start of the Green River Half Marathon in his state. I never forgot that name and recently I got the nicest note from him that read: *I am pretty sure you will not remember me, but we met at the half marathon in Green River, WY. We sat beside each other on the bus ride to the starting line. I have retold this story at least a thousand times, but I will tell it again to you.*

That half marathon was my first. I was in my early 30's, and I believe you were in your mid 60's. I was extremely nervous about the race, but you visited with me on the bus ride and kept reassuring me that it would be okay. We started the race, and of course I started way too fast. However, I was pretty happy with how the race was progressing. I had no thoughts of being anywhere near the top, but as I neared the last part of the race I knew there were many more behind me than in front of me. With about a mile left in the race, I looked back and saw you approaching. I gave absolutely everything I had, and you blew past me like I was standing still. When I finally crossed the finish line, you were there to give me words of encouragement and you introduced me to some of your family who had been out for bike rides. We both finished in the top 15, but you were quite a little ahead of me.

I have taken a lot of ribbing from my non-running friends over this story. They like to remind me of the old lady that kicked my rear. Never mind that they have no idea. You have been an inspiration for me since that time. I have now completed many half marathons and marathons, but I am still amazed by your athletic ability, and I still appreciate the kind words you had for me that day. I now make myself complete every training run with a last mile at a quicker pace, telling myself that I can't let Libby pass me.

If you ever pass through Farson, WY

Libby James

and want to go for a jog, let me know. It would
be an honor.
 Thanks again
 Trip Applequist

Thanks for having me.

Dennis Vanderheiden and Zachary Scott

Diversities and Determination

Long-time runner and triathlete Dennis
Vanderheiden knew he was through chasing
personal bests the day in 2008 when he
finished an Ironman triathlon in Louisville,
Kentucky. He figured out that his satisfaction
came not from a fast finish but from
experiencing the joy of others as they
completed an event. He would never quit
training, competing and challenging himself,

but he realized that the journey was more important to him than the finish. And he knew the journey would be enhanced if he could share it with someone unable to do it on their own. That was the day Athletes in Tandem was born, inspired by Dick Hoyt who has pushed and pulled his disabled son in numerous Hawaii Ironman races.

Athletes in Tandem recruits volunteers, supplies equipment and makes it possible for those with disabilities to participate in running, biking and swimming events. Participants have ranged in age from nine to 86.

"There's a story behind every athlete," Vanderheiden said. Many of the athletes cannot speak but sounds and gestures express their elation at feeling the wind in their hair, cool water on their bodies and kudos and camaraderie from their fellow athletes.

These days people from all over the country seek advice from Vanderheiden on how they can become involved, what equipment they need, and whether or not there is a similar organization in their area. Athletes in Tandem now has a presence in Syracuse, New York, Louisville, Kentucky and Des Moines, Iowa. There are several similar organizations in New England, California, Maryland and other states.

In 2012, a young man from Gainesville, Florida raised money for Athletes in Tandem and Wounded Warriors by doing a half ironman in Florida, then running across the

U.S. in May and June before completing his adventure with a full Ironman in Lake Tahoe, California in September. Vanderheiden joined him for the 70.3-mile Florida half Ironman with an athlete in tandem.

Dennis is supported in his work by individuals who serve on his board of directors and several local sponsors. He credits Raintree Athletic Club in Fort Collins where he works out and masseuse Sarah Hodapp for keeping him injury free. "What keeps me going is the love from parents, family members, caregivers, support organizations and friends old and new that I meet and interact with in person or on Facebook," Dennis said.

Joe Shaver can't say enough good things about Dennis Vanderheiden and Athletes in Tandem. These days Joe and his son, Logan, eight, who is autistic and unlike many disabled athletes, very mobile, often train together on the country roads east of their home in Wellington, a small town in rural Northern Colorado. Logan rides in a specially constructed stroller called a wike that fits on the back of a bike and converts easily into a running stroller.

Logan is happiest when he's out on the road. He makes noises and stomps his feet to express his pleasure. Joe says the longer the event, whether it be a training run or a race, the better Logan likes it. He's a big fan of the water as well. In fact, when he's pulled in a raft during the swim portion of a triathlon, it's a challenge to keep him in the boat. He's been known to maneuver himself overboard, causing some concern to his race partner, though it's all fun for Logan. "These activities are the way I can connect with Logan," his dad said. "It's not possible for us to share sports like wrestling, football or basketball. Dennis has been a great inspiration for the Shaver family."

"I had some hesitation at first," Logan's mom Jessica said. "Now I have great respect for what Dennis does. The first time I saw Logan's face light up during a run, I was hooked."

Joe is now in great physical shape because of the family's involvement in the program. He ran a couple of 5ks solo just to make sure he could do it before signing up to push Logan. The father and son have done 5ks, 10ks and half-marathons together.

"Whenever there's an event to benefit Athletes in Tandem, we're in," Jessica said. They have participated in the Thanksgiving Day race in Windsor, Colorado and the Pelican Fest and Lake-to-Lake triathlon in Loveland, Colorado. In January they did the Sweaty Sweater 5k and the Polar Bear Plunge companion event in the freezing waters of Horsetooth Reservoir in the foothills west of Fort Collins.

When she was 13, Destiny, Logan's older sister, ran cross-country at Wellington Middle School and completed the school's duathlon-(run-bike-run) event. The youngest Shaver, Ainsley, three-and-a-half, tags along with her family waiting her turn to join in the fun.

Katie and Jim Waechter are the parents of twins, James and Libby, 13, who were born at 29 weeks, each weighing about three pounds. Both have cerebral palsy and are unable to walk. Libby can speak. They are eighth graders and have a younger brother, Max, who is seven. They were involved with Athletes in Tandem for five years before becoming so involved in their own athletic activities that they seldom have time to enter Vanderheiden's events.

He met the family through a Special Olympics basketball program when his organization was brand new. "Dennis was so inspiring to us that we got our own adaptive equipment and began doing events on our own," Katie said. The twins have done three Horsetooth Half Marathons—one of which Katie and Jim trained for and completed along with them. The twins have also completed triathlons and a Horsetooth Reservoir swim.

Athletes in Tandem was the stepping-stone for all their athletic activity according to Katie. Her kids want to be athletes so badly that they are motivated to try most anything. They've learned to ski with adaptive equipment and look forward to learning to waterski. They both play basketball on special teams and Libby trained for and completed a 5k course alone on her bike. "It was a huge feat," Katie said. Libby's cerebral palsy prevents her from walking and affects her motor skills, making tasks that require physical coordination extremely difficult.

Katie appreciates Athletes in Tandem because it provides the opportunity for her kids to be outdoors and totally engaged in having a good time. Much of their lives revolve around doctors' appointments and various therapies, and all that can be forgotten on the road or in the water.

The Waechter family loves the selection of adaptive equipment that is available. They have walkers, a jogging stroller and a bike. A special harness hung above the treadmill in their newly remodeled basement allows Libby and James to work out in ways they could not otherwise.

The Waechters haven't deserted Athletes in Tandem, they've just been too busy to join races lately. Katie said they plan to be back— "When we can find the time," she promises.

Doug and Marji Nash

Race Across the Sky

Every one of the 798 starters at the 30th running of the Leadville Trail 100 Race Across the Sky on August 18, 2012, had a story to tell. And so did the hundreds of race organizers, volunteers, and crew members needed to make this grueling event starting at 10,200 feet a reality.

Of those who tackled the unforgiving monster at 4 a.m. on Saturday morning—a course that traverses 50 miles of high altitude Rocky Mountain terrain and then asks you to turn right around and do it again— 360 made it within the 30-hour time limit to finish and earn a belt buckle.

Those of us who haven't run this race can never know how they really felt—in their bodies and in their heads and hearts. But it was a privilege to be there, to be allowed a tiny peek as these ordinary people did an extraordinary thing.

The finishers ranged in age from 19 to 60-something. Fifty-five were women. They came from 18 countries and 41 states, and they brought with them their spouses, parents, children, dogs, friends, and gear—from special food and drink to clothing for all kinds of weather, hiking poles to navigate the tough terrain, and Tylenol to ease the pain.

The crew

As a group they represented the epitome in athleticism, discipline, willingness to hurt, love of challenge, and fierce determination. As individuals they come alive in their diversity. They are like Robert, the young "fruitarian" from Tennessee with a carful of hundreds of apples and bananas who swore his new-found diet cured the pain in his knee, or like Chris from Maryland, who hadn't a clue about altitude. He was paced by his 16-year-old son and supported by Karen, his wife. "We like to support each other's dreams," she said.

Three Fort Collins runners made the cut in 2012. Doug Nash completed his fourth LT (Leadville Trail) 100 in 29 hours 25 minutes, supported by his wife, Marji, an experienced crew manager, who made the complex route-finding, parking, re-supplying with food, drink and clothing jobs look simple when they obviously were not.

Nick Clark came in third overall in an amazing 17 hours 11 minutes. He described his major challenge. "I have to work to consume enough calories to maintain my energy level while running uphill at altitude without choking or throwing up." Alex May finished in 29 hours 42 minutes.

Once they begin the return trip from Winfield at the 50-mile mark, runners are allowed a pacer to run beside them and provide moral support, carry a water bottle, and during the night, provide extra light and watch for obstacles in the trail. A few go it alone, but most welcome the company, and pacers get a taste of what it's like out on the trail. When their 10 or so miles are done, pacers wave their runner on, thankful to be finished with their small part in the event.

For most of the participants, the sun had risen again by the time they caught sight of the relentless clock at the finish line. And most walked toward it, some more gimpy than others, accompanied by their pacers, friends and family who had lived through their runner's experience on the sidelines.

At the awards ceremony, every finisher who made the cut-off time was acknowledged and presented with the coveted silver and gold belt buckle. Like graduations, it takes a while, but like graduations, it ranks right up there with life's memorable moments.

Four years later at age 62, Doug was not finished with the LT100. During the summer of 2016, he put in countless hours, often dawn to dusk, running on the trails around Mt. Elbert. During those long runs, he trained his mind and his body to maintain a slow, steady pace that would allow him to finish in under 30 hours. His strategy paid off big time.

At seven a.m. on the morning of August 23rd, Doug had eight miles to go and was battling it out with a fellow in his age group. According to Marji, he had enough grit and stamina to pick up the pace and pull ahead by four minutes. He finished in 29 hours, three minutes and 11 seconds, good enough for third out of a 60-69 age group with 18 entrants.

Doug has run a total of six LT100s. He completed the course in 2005, 2007, 2009 and 2012. In 2014 he called it quits at mile 85. A problem called "the leans," which he had experienced for the last 50 miles in 2012, returned with a vengeance that year. "He had 15 miles to go and six hours in which to do it," Marji explained. "He was so bent over that it was impossible for him to stand upright. It wasn't safe for him to continue."

In 2016 he returned to the race confident that the summer training program he'd designed for himself would make it possible for him to avoid the leans. It worked. As one of the three top finishers in his age group he took home first LT100 trophy to add to his collection of belt buckles.

The Nashes spent the winter of 2018 in Arizona where Doug hooked up with four LT100 friends, all 64 or older, to do the 60k Black Canyon race from Spring Valley to Black Canyon City. They passed up on the 100k option in favor of the shorter distance that they referred to as a "fun run."

Spectators cheer on the runners

Libby James

The Frosting on the Cake

Some dedicated runners never compete.
Others scan upcoming events to find the
perfect race. Distance, terrain, size of race
and even the T-shirt offered can be factors.
Many runners sign up for the same few races
each year, because of tradition. They always
do that particular race. Or they sign up to
support a favorite cause. Runners choose an
"away" race in a desirable spot so they can
travel, explore a new place, and perhaps take
advantage of low altitude and runner-
friendly weather.

By the time I ran my first race, a 10k, I'd
been putting in a solid one-mile training run
almost every morning for five years. That
first race was so long ago that I no longer
remember why I decided to do it. I remember
well the sense of elation I felt afterwards. I
was flying high!

Over the years since then, I haven't kept
track of how many races I've run. I'd estimate
the number to be at least 500—all of them
fun, even the Duke City Half Marathon in
Albuquerque where I fell flat on the
pavement at mile 11 and finished dripping
blood from my elbow.

But preparing to run in a race is not the
most important incentive to get me out onto
the road. Competing in a race is an
opportunity to confront a challenge, see how

you measure up against your peers, and enjoy happy banter among friends. Yet, if I never ran another race, that fact would not change my running schedule.

It's the act of plunking one foot down in front of the other, the act of running that I love most. It helps me get a good start on the day or wind down at the end of a busy one. In winter I like foul weather that forces the body's little aches/pains/glitches to take a back seat to the business of surviving a run—and getting back home before frostbite sets in. Figuring out how to maintain an upright position while running on icy roads demands some serious concentration as well.

I appreciate the cool quiet of the early morning on a summer day that will soon become a sizzler. Rain is so rare in Colorado that running wet is a treat. Running into the wind is only fun when the wind changes and it is no longer blasting at you or when you turn around and the wind helps rather than hinders.

When I run alone, paying little or no attention to pace, all sorts of ideas pop up; some fleeting and silly, others thoughts I'm convinced I would never have had without the freedom that a solitary run provides. Daydreaming and idle looking around; there's no better time or place to do it than out on the road with no one else around.

Would running be as satisfying without the structure that the knowledge of an upcoming race provides? Every runner will have their own answer to that question. For me, the answer is "yes." While I love going to races, the challenge of testing myself against others, and the camaraderie before during and after the event, racing is not why I run.

Of course I plan training runs as I prepare for an event. But other times, I love to go out without a particular time or mileage goal and just run. I like the freedom to vary my course, find new places to go, get a little lost (That's easy for me.), and see something new. If running can be compared to cake and racing to the frosting on top, then I need a whole lot of plain cake fancied up by the addition of an occasional exciting topping

1950 nylon windbreaker

How Do I Look?

In 1972 when I began running, I did it in the dark one for fear that someone might see me doing something weird. It didn't matter at all what I wore or how I looked. Five decades later, I still don't care much about how I look when I go out for a run. But the way most runners look when they run has changed a whole lot over time.

I ran my first race in tennis shoes and my first marathon in a pair of tight-fitting knit shorts that zipped up the front and had a big pocket. No doubt my feet were better off when I invested in a pair of "real" running shoes, but the bottom half of me did just as well in a pair of ordinary shorts as it does today in high tech capri compression tights.

These days I find it fun to look a little goofy. I recently ended up with a pair of big, round, red-rimmed sunglasses. I love them because they fit well. I have a very small head and most sunglasses end up sliding down my nose.

I've been told that these red sunglasses are bad news. My daughter says they don't match anything I wear and she says they make me look silly. I've decided to take advantage of this assessment and wear them every time I run. I also make a concerted effort to speak to every runner I pass, wishing them good morning, or whatever is appropriate, and watching to see if they reply, and if they smile.

One of my best running buddies likes to match her clothes, right down to her socks. I make a conscious effort to *not* match. I don't have to think much about what I put on while she plans carefully so that she looks, well, all matched up.

When you get right down to it, all you really need for running is a good pair of shoes. But it is possible to arrive at the starting line decked out in pink compression arm sleeves, Nike Pro combat compression tights, plus, if you are a woman, a skinny little running dress. Beneath it all you could be wearing Under Armor panties and a shock absorber bra. If you have to ask what this kind getup might cost you, then you don't really need any of it.

Comfort counts most. Make sure your shoes fit well and the laces stay tied, even if you have to tie double knots. Replace your shoes when they break down to avoid injury. Wear socks that are thick enough to provide some padding. Make sure shorts or tights don't rub in the wrong places, and layer shirts to be prepared for changing weather. A hat or visor makes sense for protection from high-altitude sunshine. Wimps like me usually start out with gloves in cool weather, and shed them after a mile or so. At the very least they come in handy for wiping a drippy nose.

And don't forget to wear a pair of goofy-looking sunglasses.

Big red sunglasses

Dan Berlin and Connie

Connie Loves to Run

She loves to run, and she loves numbers.
Three years ago, Connie DeMercurio, by day
Special Projects Coordinator for a non-profit
that assists single mothers, signed on as
treasurer of the Fort Collins Running Club.
Before she knew it, she had been elected
president. By her second year in office, her
contagious enthusiasm generated some
impressive numbers. The club grew from 100
to 200 members and attendance at its

monthly predict races soared from 10 to 90 participants.

Connie's devotion to her favorite sport extends beyond the personal satisfaction she derives from running. She devotes lots of time to encouraging others to discover its joys. For three years she faithfully guided blind runner Dan Berlin through marathons in New York, Boston, Washington D. C., Fort Collins and Denver. She has been active in Athletes in Tandem, pushing a stroller carrying someone unable to run because of a disability. The epitome of those experiences came last September when she pushed a 90-pound man in a stroller and *at the same time* guided Dan through the Crossroads Half Marathon in Fort Collins.

Connie and Dan have become a smooth-running team. They talk to each other often as they run, and in crowded situations, as in the New York Marathon, are tethered together. Other times Connie runs a little ahead and Dan follows, using his ability to see white lines and contrasts. Connie has learned to wear bright clothing so Dan can see her better. Dan's trust in her, his changed diet, weight loss, and added muscle have resulted in faster times and opened up a whole new world to him. There was a time when running with Dan meant a sacrifice of time for Connie, but no longer.

Growing up in the Chicago area and in Santa Barbara, California, Connie confesses to being a couch potato until age 21 when she discovered swimming. After insisting to Doug, her runner husband, that she hated running, she took up the sport anyway at age 30 because it was the most convenient way to work out after delivering her daughter to a pre-school that happened to be close to a running trail.

In 1989 she entered the 10k Colorado Run in her hometown of Fort Collins. The race was held on Labor Day and at that time the race awarded women who finished under 48 minutes a special long-sleeved shirt. She earned one. Since then she has clocked the fastest half-marathon in the state in her 55-59 age group with a 1:33 at Georgetown, Colorado in 2012, and completed a 3:18:36 marathon in Napa Valley, California at age 54.

"She gets faster as she gets older, " says daughter Marissa, herself a veteran of three marathons. She and Connie did the Chicago Marathon together. Marissa's brother, Nate, ran the Marine Corps Marathon with his mother and has completed a 50-mile race, two half Ironmans, and met the challenge of a full Ironman. Despite an ailing knee, Connie guided Dan through the Marine Corps Marathon in October 2012, chalking up her 28th time at that distance.

Connie's love of numbers doesn't extend to tracking her times in shorter races or her annual mileage. "It's not important. I just love to run," she says. "I love the beauty of it, the companionship, the opportunity to explore new places, and it makes me feel good."

In the last five years, Connie has run five marathons and has plans for a half marathon and two more full marathons in 2018 which she will schedule in between visits to Texas to spend time with two small grandchildren.

Erica Burr with Daughters Maddie and
Isabelle

Running When Kids are Small: Making it Work

Question: Can a young mom with two small
children, a husband who travels, and a
demanding full-time job maintain a satisfying
running schedule?

"Yes," said Erica Burr, "but you have to get
creative."

I've been watching Erica for several years
now, from the time when her first child was a
toddler through the birth of a second
daughter until today, as her daughters are
growing up.

Active in volleyball, basketball, and track
during high school, Erica began to run
regularly as a freshman at Northern Illinois

University, and it has been an important part of her life ever since. She remembers Midwest winds so strong that she had to run backwards to get home.

A visit to Fort Collins with a friend during college and all the runners she saw in the area made her decide to move west after graduation in 1997. A degree in English and experience in web development landed her a marketing coordinator position at Hewlett Packard where she met Chris, a software engineer. They married in 2002.

In the days before their daughter Maddie arrived in 2006, Erica and Chris often trained and did races together. "HP had showers on site and back then dirt roads surrounded the place. It was easy to get in a good run at noon," Erica said. Exercise has gotten more complicated for Erica since those days.

For six months after Maddie was born, Erica ran pushing Maddie in a regular stroller. It didn't work well. "A jogging stroller was the best investment I ever made. Maddie lived in it," Erica said. When she got old enough to choose, Erica would offer Maddie a nap or a ride in the stroller. She seldom chose to stay at home.

Erica established a routine that allowed her to run 20 miles a week, about half those miles on the weekends. Because Chris traveled every other week, Erica hired a girl twice a week on those weeks, to come to her home about 6:45 a.m. and get Maddie ready for daycare. Erica was working at Colorado State University at the time and lived close enough to ride her bike to work. At 3 p.m. she biked home, changed her clothes and ran to Maddie's daycare where she retrieved her for a four-mile run in the jogging stroller.

"As Maddie got a little older, there were times when she balked," Erica said. "I told her that making it possible for me to run is something she is doing for me and that it is not a choice." Erica's father has diabetes and she is convinced that running will help her maintain a healthy lifestyle. When she was six, Maddie ran her first 5k, struggling a bit during the race, but full of pride afterwards.

Isabelle came along in 2009 and the stroller had a new occupant. Before long Maddie was able to bike alongside Erica as she ran with Isabelle.

The girls are older now. At age 11, Maddie is allowed to choose whether or not she will run with Erica. She usually goes. Isabelle goes on her bike.

Occasionally Erica is able to sneak away from work and get in a run at noon. "There isn't a shower available, but I manage. The important thing is getting in the run," she says.

Erica still manages to clock 20 miles a week, sometimes a bit more. "If I get lucky." The family now lives outside of town in an area where she runs along a canal behind her house. "Sometimes the girls come with me, but honestly, I prefer to run alone, early in the morning. I head out at 6 a.m. During the winter months I run most mornings in the dark. I prefer morning because it is more peaceful and quiet. It is my sacred alone time. Also, I know that if I try to do it later in the day, it might not happen. Between the kids and work, there is just too much going on in the afternoon."

These days Erica is more comfortable on her early runs when her little dog, Charlotte, goes along. On the days when the early run doesn't work out, Isabelle accompanies Erica on her bike in the afternoon after school and work. Sometimes she's a little grumpy at the start but always enjoys herself after a few minutes, according to Erica.

Maddie ran cross-country as a sixth grader, finishing 15th out of 201 girls at the district meet. Erica raced once in 2017, coming in 10th in her age group at the inaugural running of the Fortitude 10k race in Fort Collins. For now, family takes priority, but Erica looks forward to devoting more time to running in the future.

"It is my stress reliever, fitness and weight management tool, the activity that gets me outside," she says. She has encountered coyotes, bald eagles, hawks, deer, a mountain lion, a king fisher and blue heron on the path where she runs. She looks forward to the challenge of running in crazy weather, once spotting a bald eagle flying into a 40-mile an hour wind about 10 feet from her. "It made running in the miserable wind worthwhile," she said. "It was like the bird was rewarding me for coming out and giving me the strength to keep going. I know running is a part of me and always will be."

Exploring the Studies

Like political polls, study results can be misleading, hard to believe, depressing, or downright silly. Gretchen Reynolds, who writes a running column for the *New York Times,* often quotes study results. Some offer something to ponder, confirm what you already know, and sometimes even share new and useful information. Here's what some of the studies say:

Marathons rarely kill. An article in the May 2012 *American Journal of Sports Medicine* revealed that between 1999 and 2009 the number of marathon finishers in a year rose from 299,000 to 472,000 but the death rate remained the same—less than one per 100,000 participants. Twenty-eight people died during or in the 24 hours after a marathon, mostly men with heart problems. A few died from low blood sodium caused by drinking too many liquids.

The January 2012 *New England Journal of Medicine* confirms what cardiologist Dr. Paul Thompson, already believed: "You are at slightly higher risk of suffering a heart attack during a marathon than if you were sitting or walking during those same hours. But overall, running decreases the risk of heart disease. Genetics, viruses, and bad habits from the past can cause development of plaque in the heart arteries and enlargement of the heart muscle which running cannot prevent."

The doctor, who was forced to quit running because of a bad hip said: "I ran marathons because I loved them, not because I expected them to help me live forever. I don't know if it's the healthiest way to spend years of your life. But it was enjoyable. I miss running very, very much."

A recent study at the University of South Carolina Arnold School of Public Health offers good news for the slow and steady. Researchers found that running in moderation provided the most benefits. People who logged up to 20 miles a week at about 10 or 11 minutes per mile pace reduced their risk of dying compared to people who did not run and also compared to those who ran more than 20 miles a week, or who ran faster than seven miles an hour. About 20 miles of running a week appears to provide the best protection from mortality risk. "More is not better, and can be worse," says Dr. Carl J. Lavie. "Run more if you like, but only if you don't experience extreme fatigue or frequent injuries."

Researchers at the University of Arizona wondered why our ancestors continued to run over time rather than developing other strategies for survival. Perhaps it is because running makes human beings feel good. Blood samples from humans and dogs after they had run for 30 minutes, showed increased levels of a naturally occurring cannabis-like chemical that alters and lightens mood. After 30 minutes of walking, no such increase occurred. When ferrets were encouraged to run (which they did with difficulty), their blood samples showed no change in endocannabinoid levels. Conclusion: Humans are hard-wired to run, ferrets are not.

A study of Western adults reported that every hour of television viewing after age 25 lowers life expectancy by 21.8 minutes. Our physical activity can affect how long, and more importantly, how well we live. All the studies tell us so. No exercise prevents aging, one wise expert noted. "Only death can do that."

Another study, published in the *Proceedings of the National Academy of Science* and reported in the June 2015 issue of *Double Runner* magazine addressed the behaviors of people referred to as niners, those on the cusp of entering a new decade in their lives. If you happen to be a niner, here's a little information that may interest you. When you become 29, 39, 49, 59 or better, beware. According to this study, niners are more likely to "run a marathon, have an affair, commit suicide or take part in other behaviors that reflect an ongoing search for meaning."

These behaviors, the article by Laura Young, MD continues, can cause either constructive or destructive behavior as people reflect on the upcoming new decade in their lives. A series of six studies looked at people in 100 countries and found that these

behaviors were more prevalent among niners
world-wide.

The study used data from *Athlinks.com* to
learn about the behavior of runners. They
found that an exceptionally high percentage
of first-time marathoners were niners.
Statistics also showed that road runners
posted times more than two percent faster as
niners than they were able to run in the two
years before or after their niner year.

So what's all this about? Perhaps it is
logical that runners might up their mileage
and train a bit harder in anticipation of
entering a new age group where they will
have the advantage of being among the
youngest in the division. Is this niner issue
something we all recognize, anticipate and
acknowledge, or is it a subconscious thing?

Are we better off to embrace this
phenomenon or blow it off as a silly notion?
Since it is going to arrive anyway for all of us,
perhaps it makes sense to use it for good.
Instead of having an affair, offer your partner
or spouse a little special attention. Instead of
vegging out in front of the TV, see if you can't
incorporate a couple more miles into your
weekly training schedule. And if you've never
addressed the challenge of running a
marathon, maybe this is the year to give it a
go. The same applies to running in a race or
attempting a challenging hike or bike ride.

It's interesting to think about what
motivates human beings to decide to do
difficult things. Setting a goal is important.
With a specific goal in mind, it matters less

how uncomfortable, expensive, scary or time-consuming the preparation may be. Making some sort of sacrifice becomes a part of the commitment.

It would be interesting to know the ages of individuals when they rowed solo across an ocean, climbed Mr. Everest or jumped out of an airplane. There's an opportunity for a Ph.D dissertation.

I entered my niner year forewarned by the results of the study. I got through the year without doing anything crazy. I celebrated leaving the niners with an out-of-the-ordinarily-hard four-mile run, not long but heavy on altitude gain. I was happy that I could keep pace with the family members that went along. It was a good way to say good-bye to my status as a niner.

The next morning I delivered the last of a group which included my children, their spouses and several grandkids, to the airport and back to their various lives. These "kids" came from New York, San Diego, Seattle, Washington D.C., Tokyo, Cheyenne, Orlando and Fort Collins, to celebrate my birthday. I love them for being willing to do that. I love them even more for the extreme hilarity they generate when they get together. A little nightlife, some Frisbee, swimming, silly games—they did it all—and then they went away.

It was pretty quiet at my house after they left. Don't get me wrong. I relished the quiet and the time to reminisce a bit, to appreciate all the good times of the last few days. So many great memories.

And then it was time to embrace a new decade and sign up for a race in a new age group. It was good to know that I didn't need to worry about contemplating any erratic behavior for another nine years.

The Magic Kingdom in the dark

Disney's Princess Half Marathon

On the side of the road lay a blue-green tutu, tossed aside by a would-be princess.

It's not easy becoming a princess and that includes dressing up as if you were one. Especially not when you must be all decked out before 4 a.m. on a misty, moisty Florida morning in order to wait around in a "corral" for an hour plus before you begin a 13.1 mile run along with 22,000 other princess wannabees.

Not until a booming male voice has belted out the national anthem and your slightly overweight and extraordinarily cheery fairy godmother has intoned "salagadula means, michakabularu" from a stage at the starting line are you released into the dark to "live your dream" any way you can manage it.

I'm a little chagrined to say that my daughter Kristin and I ran the Disney Princess Half Marathon in Orlando sans tutu, tiara, feather boa, and face sparkles. In the hours before the race began, it became obvious that as the unadorned, we were part of a small and obvious minority. Even most of the thousand-plus men who ran this female-focused race got into the act with fancy shirts and an occasional tiara or feather boa.

Kristin and I don't go in much for "fru-fru" but both of us emerged from this elaborately staged race with a whole new set of insights. We came to admire the fact that so many of the 20,000-plus participants were doing their very first half-marathon. I'm fairly certain that more than a few of them suspected they would struggle to complete the race in the allotted time, (an average of 16-minute miles) but that wasn't stopping any of them.

One radiant young woman approached me to explain that this was her first half marathon and she was six weeks out from a double mastectomy. Another had been dealing with diabetes since childhood. Less than a mile from the finish, I saw a runner stop to help a fellow runner who was limping—barely able to move forward.

Instead of allowing this girl to struggle on alone, the runner sacrificed her very respectable pace to help. "Come on," I heard her say. "We'll finish this thing together."

It was kind of a fluke that I ended up running the Disney Princess Half. Five weeks before I'd run in the Disney World Half Marathon on the very same course through Epcot and the Magic Kingdom. It was the first race I'd ever chosen specifically to see if I could set an age-group American record on a certified course. I chose this one because Disney would never put on a race that wasn't fully certified and also because my younger son, Jeff and his family live in Orlando.

I had the good fortune to set the record I was shooting for, and that fact resulted in a most generous offer to return with a companion, all expenses paid, to speak on a couple of panels and run the Princess Half if I'd like to. I was thrilled to be able to invite my daughter from Cheyenne, Wyoming, to come with me.

Look askance all you wish at runners adorned in capes, crowns, feathers and glitters. The hard fact remains that 13.1 miles is 13.1 miles, and there is no easy, pain-free way to get the job done.

I know for certain that at least one runner had to toss her blue-green tutu aside to complete the race. She was no less a princess because of that.

A reward at the end of the race

A Challenge Every Year

April 12:

On a Friday afternoon off from her job as head of the Citizen Information Center in Larimer County Courthouse in Fort Collins, Colorado, Gael Cookman headed out the door to run 11 miles. In three weeks she would crank up her run to 13.1 miles when she lined up to run the Colorado Half Marathon down Poudre Canyon west of Fort Collins in her first-ever race at that distance.

Gael, mother of three, sole supporter of her family and veteran of 23 years of military service, was no stranger to challenge or to managing her time. In addition to her full-time job for the County, she was regional vice president and an independent consultant for Arbonne, a cosmetics firm. A couple of times a week she taught spinning classes at a local health club.

This energetic lady makes it a point to do something for the first time every year. Firsts have included the Bolder Boulder 10k, snowboarding, and learning to play golf. "I tell people in my spinning classes how important it is to reach outside your comfort zone," Gael said. In this, the year she turned 50, she chose to do a half-marathon with the goal of finishing in less than two hours.

Years ago she had competed in shorter races, and while stationed in Germany in the service, she trained for the Berlin Marathon. But duty called her away and she was unable to participate.

Gael thrived on a training program that pushed her to increase her mileage by the week and included a weekly long run. She did intervals, added a few carbohydrates to an already healthy diet, and was careful not to overdo her training in order to stay injury-free. She became conscientious about limiting sweets but could not be talked out of the benefits of a glass of red wine in the evening.

The things she found most challenging were finding the time to train and dealing with unpredictable weather. Fortunately, there's a shower in the courthouse which allowed Gael to go for a run during her lunch hour and return to work presentable.

A people person, Gael has a wide circle of friends, but she chose to do her training runs alone. "It's my time to unwind, meditate and regenerate," she said. She's enjoyed the challenge of meeting weekly mileage goals, though she admitted that the long runs were tiring. The hint of a stress fracture showed up during her training but soon disappeared, much to her relief.

May 5: "Perfect timing," Gael said as she answered my phone call. "I just woke up from a nap. The race was amazing. Hard. Freezing at the start. Thank goodness for a trash bag for warmth. Right now, I'm not sure I'd do it again, but I loved it."

Gael's muscles, cold and stiff from standing around for an hour at the starting line, loosened up after the first few miles of running down the canyon, only to be replaced by a strange twinge in her right knee at mile five. But it disappeared a few miles down the road.

Even though they trained solo, Gael and her friend, Melissa Dasakis, stayed together for the first 12 miles of the race. "Melissa has done lots of races, including marathons, and she was a great support for me," Gael said.

Near the end of the race they parted, each zeroed in on giving it all they had left. Melissa finished less than a minute ahead of Gael whose time, one hour, 58 minutes and 29 seconds. She had accomplished her goal with time to spare and earned a fifth place finish in her age group.

"This evening," Gael said, as we ended our phone visit, "that glass of red wine is looking better than ever. I think I earned it."

Libby James

First grade teacher Payton Schneider

Two Teachers Inspire Young Runners

As soon as school was out the summer of
2013, two Cache La Poudre Elementary
School teachers in the small town of LaPorte,
Colorado, made a plan. They would meet
three times a week all summer to run
together. They benefitted so much from the
experience that when school resumed in the
fall, they wanted to find a way to share the
joy they had discovered in running with their
students.

Leslie Glenn and Payton Schneider invited students from all grades to join them after school twice a week for a run. Fortunately, there was a leafy trail along the Poudre River behind their school, leading to a bridge that became a convenient turn-around point.

The teachers were happy with a turnout of 20 students that first year. They planned two six-week sessions, one in the fall and another in the spring. The Cache LaPoudre Running Club has flourished. At the spring sign-up, 50 kids appeared. Thirty-five of them, along with Schneider and Glenn, participated in the Hunger Pains 5k, in April, an event organized by a local high school student to benefit the local county food bank.

The running club is a free after school activity open to all, kindergarten through grade five. Parents of the littlest ones, kindergarteners through second grade, run alongside their children. "It's become a social time for the parents," Payton said.

Workouts begin with stretches in the gym before everyone heads out the door to the path behind the school. There's never any pressure. Kids tend to take off at great speed and pretty soon peter out. That's fine. Walking is encouraged whenever needed. Stronger runners are free to extend their run beyond the Poudre River Bridge and gauge their turnaround time so that everyone is back at school by 4:30.

"Ideally we'd like to meet twice a week," Glenn explained. But both teachers have young children and struggle to find after-school time that often.

On a May afternoon, I joined 40-plus kids, four teachers and several parents on their afternoon run. Most had running shoes, but an occasional kid trucked along in flip-flops or Crocs, not one bit concerned about their footwear. The feeling was festive. Everyone felt happy. School was out for the day. The weather was warm and these kids were moving along together, enjoying the outdoors, laughing, joking and chatting with each other.

A note I received after that run made me realize how much impact the Cache La Poudre Running Club has had on its participants. It read:

Hi Libby,

I'm Ryan's mom. Thank you for running with the club yesterday and talking to the kids about running. I want to tell you how much the club has impacted our family. It has made Ryan a runner. Mrs. Schneider and Mr. Strutz noticed his talent and suggested he start racing. Last year's Hunger Pains was his first-ever 5k. He beat the teachers and he loved the race.

Ryan ran several more races over the summer. He had pneumonia when he was young followed by sports-induced asthma. Luckily he has outgrown the asthma, but it still amazes me that he does 5ks.

Running has given Ryan power over being small for his age. He's been picked on and has always hated any reference to "short." Now he shocks runners as he passes them. He's heard them call out, "Way to go little dude." These days he wears that title proudly and takes any name calling in stride.

I am so thankful for the CLP Running Club and the teachers who give their time to share the experience of running with kids.
Thanks,
Deb Lippert

In 2013 Ryan Lippert ran the Hunger Pains 5k as a fifth grader. In 2018 he competes on his high school track team.

CLP runners

John Hagin

One Hundred Marathons and No More Counting

John Hagin came painfully close to finishing his twelfth Boston Marathon on April 15, 2013. A police barricade forced him to stop shortly after the 25-mile mark and wind his way another three miles on his weary feet to his hotel near the finish line.

His wife, Woody, by now a veteran spectator, departed from her usual routine of shopping for a while and then waiting for John at the finish. This year she'd beat the crowds and make sure she had a prime viewing spot by walking a half-mile or so along the edge of the course to find a vacant spot next to the railing that separates runners from spectators. "It was the first time ever that I was not at the finish line to meet John," Woody said. That decision may have saved her life.

One of the lucky few able to reach his hotel after the race was stopped, a keyless John talked a sobbing maid into opening his room for him. It wasn't until he turned the television on that he understood why the maid was so upset. Grabbing his cell phone, he frantically called Woody, only to discover that he could not get through to her.

Thus began a seven-hour saga for the couple who were eventually reunited at their hotel after dark. By then John had showered and was resting on the bed.

"Rotten guy," was Woody's comment when she finally found her way to their hotel room. Those words were followed by a hug and an enormous sense of relief.

John ran the race, but it was Woody who experienced the full impact of the chaos caused by the explosion of two pressure-cooker bombs near the finish line of the 117th Boston Marathon. She heard shattering booms, then saw police running toward the finish, ambulances, cops on bikes, SWAT teams and crowds of frightened people who'd been told to evacuate but weren't sure where to turn. Rumors were rampant concerning the likelihood of more bombs. The whole focus appeared to be on the safety of the runners.

When Woody tried to buy a charger for her dying cell phone, she discovered that a SWAT team member had purchased every charger in the store. For a very long time, she

Woody and John Hagin

walked the streets aimlessly wondering what to do. She hadn't eaten all day. A lonely meal at the Cheesecake Factory seemed a far cry from the celebratory dinner she and John had planned. As daylight disappeared, she discovered a back way in to her hotel by sneaking through a small opening in the yellow tape delineating a crime scene.

John has been running since the early '70s when he weighed 200 pounds and a doctor told him to change his ways or die. He stopped counting marathons when he'd completed more than 100. He's done every event possible in Leadville, Colorado, altitude 10,200 feet, from a 100-mile trail run to a 10k. He's run almost every day since he began except for three weeks off to heal a broken leg.

These days, at age 72, John puts in 35 to 40 miles a week and insists he doesn't train. "I just run," he says. He couldn't think of a better birthday gift for Woody than to present her with an entry into the Hawaii Marathon. She ran it, her first, on the day she turned 50.

Shortly after they came home from Boston, Woody and John reserved a room in a Boston hotel for the 2014 running of the race. They felt it was important to make a statement in that way. That year John finished in four hours and ten minutes and has returned to run the race every year since, bringing his Boston total to 16. But in 2018 he wasn't there. He has decided to return to run the race every five years for as long as he can.

In 2017 John clocked a little over 2,000 miles on the road. He's looking forward to completing two or three marathons in the coming year, to include the San Diego Rock 'n Roll where he is a legacy runner, meaning that he has completed every race since its beginning in 1998. That year he competed three months after dealing with a cancer scare.

In the ultra distance department, John has a 50k race on his schedule. That completed, he says, he will be up for the challenge of a 100k event in the summer of 2018. Age may have slowed his pace but not his commitment to the road.

Doubles runners

Two Races in One: The Double Road Race

On July 21, 2013 a contingent of Fort Collins runners participated in the Double Road Race in Denver. It was the first Double ever staged in Colorado and only the third ever held in the U.S.A.

So what is a double? Take it from some of us who made the trip to Denver City Park for the event. It's hard. It's fun. All of us would like to do another one. In this event, you run a 10k course, pause for an intermission, and then run a 5k race. Sounds simple enough until you give it a try.

Bob Anderson, founder of *Runners World* magazine, has done several doubles and said he has learned something new every time he's done one. The concept of the double is his, and he has the innovative spirit, organizational savvy and wherewithal to turn his idea into an event that could become as popular as any 10k race or half-marathon in the country.

Bob described the Double as something like a triathlon only different. It's a two-stage race in which competitors don't switch from swimming to cycling to running; they just run. The second leg, the 5k race, starts one hour and 45 minutes after the 10k start. That means the faster you run the 10k, the more rest time you get before you start the 5k.

During the recovery period between runs, there are all sorts of options: You can visit an on-site chiropractor or massage therapist, roll around on a foam roller, drink, eat, walk, go to the bathroom or simply sit or lie down and rest. The trick lies in figuring out what is the best way to recover and prepare for segment two. It's different for everyone. The only way to find out is to practice during training.

The founding organization has published a runners' guide to the double road race. It lists training ideas and 25 strategies you can experiment with.

Denver race director, Tyler McCandless of Boulder, is one of the nation's finest long distance runners. He encouraged an elite field to participate in the inaugural Colorado race. Tyler is a veteran of the Double. He ran in the first race in America in Pleasanton, California, finishing third with an aggregate time of 47:13 and in Overland, Kansas where he set a men's world record in 45:15:05.

The Pleasanton race attracted more than 1,000 runners and was won by Fernando

Cabada of Boulder and Tina Kekalas of
Hillsborogh, California. Molly Printz who
trains in Boulder and won in Kansas, holds
the women's record with a time of 53:13:04.

Tyler elected to run in the children's one-
mile event in Denver. "Halfway through the
race a young girl stopped to let him know
that this was her first race ever," Tyler said.

The double is for everybody, from
beginners to old-timers with an unusual
emphasis on runners 40 and over. There's
prize money three deep in 10-year age
groups and an age-graded scale with prize
money that helps to even the playing field for
the oldsters.

These days most Doubles are run in
California, Bob Anderson's home territory.
It's worth a trip to California, and if a Double
is scheduled close to home, don't miss it.

Dave Klibbe back on the road

Coming Back

On Memorial Day, 2013, Dave Klibbe was anxious to see what his new hip could do. He was hoping to run a 5k race in less than 24 minutes.

In the fall of 2012 he had his hip replaced, in hopes that one day he would be able to run pain-free. He had suffered for years with an arthritic situation that eventually resulted in a hairline hip fracture from the impact of bone on bone. Surgery seemed his only option.

Two days before the surgery, he ran a 5k race in 24 minutes, 15 seconds. For good measure, and perhaps for good luck, he ran six miles the following day. That could well have been his last run. But six months and a whole lot of hard work later, he stepped out his front door for his first post-surgery run. "It felt weird," he said. "I couldn't get any sort of rhythm going. But it felt so good to be out there. When I paused at a traffic light, tears of thankfulness running down my face, a woman turned to me and asked if I was all right. My answer was yes."

He was so elated to be accomplishing any forward motion on his own two feet without the pain he'd become so accustomed to that he kept running, a little farther and a little faster each time he went out. Eight months after surgery, he completed a 5k in 24:39. In July he ran the Double Road Race (a 10k followed by a 5k) in Denver with times of 55:29 and 28:38 and the Human Race 5k in Fort Collins in 24:20.

Dave was able to return to running because he wanted it so badly and because of help from several skilled professionals. Through his local orthopedist, Dr. Steven Yemm, Dave learned about Dr. James Rector in Boulder, the only doctor in Colorado who performs a special procedure called Birmingham Hip Resurfacing. Two days after surgery, Dave went home on a single crutch and with manageable pain. After two weeks, he was off pain medication and had begun physical therapy.

He dedicated himself 100 percent to working with Brad Ott at Rebound Physical Therapy in Fort Collins. "When I was exhausted, Brad would say, 'Give me five more.' and I would," Dave said.

"I had no idea how much my leg had suffered from running on a bad hip. I began learning how to activate the proper muscles and develop balance, muscle control and strength. After four weeks, I biked 20 miles and hiked five easy miles. By three months, my limp had disappeared. I was sleeping all night and could drive without pain. I could trim my toenails and put on my shoes pain-free."

When Dr. Rector gave Dave the go-ahead to begin running six months after surgery, he began more intensive physical therapy workouts. Brad checked him for symmetry and any favoring of the reconstructed hip. He was not able to distinguish any difference between the repaired hip and the healthy one. Through months of physical therapy, Dave learned a great deal about his body, knowledge that has made him a more aware and better runner.

Is this guy superman? Maybe a little crazy? He'd say "no" to question one and a "maybe" to question two. He is incredibly grateful to be back on the road, continuing a running habit that began when he was 35, and has become a routine he is willing to work hard to maintain.

He accomplished that sub-24-minute 5k goal running a 23.05 5k at the Festival of Races in Syracuse, New York in October 2014. In 2015 he hiked 85 miles of the Coast to Coast path in the United Kingdom in six days. In 2017 he hiked the remaining 108 miles to complete the second half of the Coast to Coast path. Later that summer he was the lead runner in a Wild West Relay team, breezing through three run segments, one of which had the steepest altitude gain in the 200-mile event.

"These days my knees are the determining factor in how much I can run," Dave said. His orthopedist and good friend, Dr. Steve Yemm has him on a program of injections in both knees every six months. "They have worked well as I search for what Steve calls 'the sweet spot' that allows me to keep running. I rely on Steve and physical therapy from Brad for what ails me. I turned 70 last year with mixed feelings; getting old versus entering a new age group."

Dave continues to run every other day and puts in several miles walking with his dog every day. He hikes, snowshoes and bikes and his hip never complains. A recent five-year check-up from Dr. Rector affirmed the health of his resurfaced hip.

Dave and I have been running together at least once a week for about five years. He pushes me and when I have a good race, he likes to claim the credit. "We have proved to be good medicine for each other," he says. "We have run three Bolder Boulder 10ks together and look forward to doing more." Dave's time in those races has been fast enough to earn him a key chain as one of the top 15 finishers in his age group. He doesn't plan on hanging up his running shoes any time soon.

Shirts bring back memories

It's All About the Shirt

To run, all you *really* need is a pair of shoes. And a few runners even skip the shoes.

But with the possible exception of the Bay to Breakers race in California where nudity and/or body paint sometimes suffices, it is traditional to cover certain essential body parts, with well, something.

Runners are on their own to purchase pants, but the T-shirts they wear are another story. Since the early days of the running boom, T-shirts have been the souvenir almost always included in the price of a race entry fee. And runners love them.

In a recent scientific survey conducted among a group of seasoned runners, I learned that runners favor "tech" or synthetic lightweight fabric T-shirts over cotton, the fabric of choice for many years. Runners say tech shirts fit better, don't get smelly, "breathe," have a nicer texture and stretch enough to "cover a car" according to one respondent. The few who favor cotton complain that tech shirts smell funny and don't fit well.

Runner people own anywhere from a couple dozen to a couple hundred shirts and know how T-shirts have a habit of accumulating in dresser drawers making those who race collectors by default. Some rotate through their shirts as they train and race, others have old favorites they prefer to wear over and over. Favorites become loved because of color, logo, fit, fabric, and "how I look in it." Sometimes they recall an especially difficult race, a memorable travel experience, or provide the owner with a not-so-subtle way to brag about having completed a status race such as the Boston Marathon.

Fit is an on-going issue. "Unisex sizing means men's sizes," one small runner says. "Even a small men's shirt becomes a nightgown for me. If race organizers want me to wear their shirt to advertise their race, then I need to have one that fits." Women runners appreciate women's sizing and tapered shirts that fit them better. Several runners appreciated a "no shirt" option to pay a lower entry fee, not very common these days.

T-shirts can create a bond between strangers who strike up a conversation based on a shirt. It's fun to learn when and where a race took place, and whether or not the experience was good. "When I wear my 'Alaska, Land of the Midnight Run' shirt I often hear 'Go Alaska,'" one runner shared.

What happens when T-shirt storage capacity is maxed out? Shirts get thrown away, given away, cut up for rags, transformed into quilts, or they find new life when sold on the streets of third world countries around the world. They arrive in huge bundles and sell for pennies. I once saw a young man in Maputo, the capital of Mozambique, proudly displaying a shirt that read, "Detroit Dance Marathon, 1995." I don't think he was in attendance.

Occasionally races offer hats, socks, a bag, jacket or sweatshirt instead of a T-shirt as a race souvenir. And sometimes runners appreciate a change. But in the end, it's the T-shirt most race participants covet and that can even become a factor in deciding whether or not to participate in a race.

A blessing or a curse, T-shirts are here to stay.

Run and Think. Think and Run.

I still own a textbook I used in college titled *Writing and Thinking: A Handbook of Composition and Revision.* The preface says the book is designed to help the college student, "improve his ability to communicate." The authors say most freshmen need extensive training in "thinking soundly," implying that learning to think soundly will help you write better.

It's been a long time since I looked at that textbook that addresses grammar, punctuation, mechanics, spelling, diction, unity, clearness and emphasis. I know I'd never read the preface before. I've done my share of writing, requiring thinking, hopefully sometimes sound. Over time I've decided that running may well be a better road to sound thinking—and in coming up with bright ideas—even better than the words in a textbook.

Often when I'm running, an idea pops up that I am determined to remember. In an attempt to hang on to my ideas--which are sometimes as simple as remembering all the things I need to do in the next couple of days--I've developed a mental filing system that I use when I run.

I alphabetize the thoughts in my head, then ask my brain to remember, not each idea, but the letter with which each idea starts. So I arrive back at my doorstep mumbling C, D, R, P. Then all I have to do is remember what each of those letters stands for! *She's nuts,* you're thinking. Probably.

There is something about the rhythm that develops over the course of a run that allows you to unhook from whatever issue was churning around in your head when you stepped out the door. Often, I leave home thinking I can only be gone for a certain number of minutes because.... And then after I've been running for a while, that project I thought I had to tackle by 10:30 can suddenly wait until noon or so. How could it possibly matter?

Running isn't the only way to disconnect from the everyday, to allow the free flow of ideas, to encourage thinking—whether it be sound, kooky, or just plain crazy off-the-wall stuff, but it is a way that works for me.

Now, I'm going for a run, and I'll reserve the last few words here to let you know what great idea emerged—hopefully before too many miles have gone by.

It happened at mile three as I passed a ditch that a couple of weeks ago had been a raging torrent. Today the water was so still that it was tinged with the green of stagnation. A little farther on, in an open space west of town, the silence was deafening. No helicopters overhead, no heavy machinery rumbling by. Mother Nature was into Colorado blue sky and sunshine; calm for the moment.

No alphabetized list emerged during my

run today. But I did realize that sometimes I write to earn myself a run and sometimes I run to help me "think soundly" as I write.

Maybe Congress could benefit from a group run.

Friends celebrating after a run

Running with Friends

I usually run alone, but I treasure the friends I've made through running, and I love to run with them. Many of them who run together regularly were kind enough to tell me why they often choose to run with others.

"My running friends get me out in the morning. I love being social, exercising, and being accountable to show up. We meet year round and help each other train for big events."

One friend quoted runner, physician and author, George Sheehan: "The reason we race isn't to BEAT each other, it's just to BE with each other."

"I am a fair weather runner who loves the support and structure of having to meet a group of runners at a specific time and place. This has helped me complete eight marathons. I've been running with a dozen runners of varying abilities for nine years. They have become some of my best friends. We've celebrated weddings, births and birthdays, and we've been there for each other through illnesses. I like larger groups so that a running partner is guaranteed when you show up at 5:30 a.m. or when it's 90 degrees outside."

"The best part of running with a group is that you commit because they are expecting you. The bonding and conversation are great. With a group, I think you sometimes put more effort into your running."

"Running in a group challenges you to try new trails and learn to maintain a pace when you are tired. The wonderful relationships that build go beyond running and become a source of encouragement and support in our lives."

"Group running has helped me to improve. It has allowed me to meet women in different stages and walks of life. Within six months of joining, I ran my first half-marathon. I'm hooked. Having a group that meets regularly has pushed me farther than I thought possible. It's easier to get out of bed when people are expecting you. Runs go more easily when you're visiting with others."

"Group running encourages easy conversation. We consider what we say before we speak—you can't be longwinded when you're trying to breathe and watch your step as well. Energy and effort multiplies when we are together. Twelve years ago I met a friend at Runners Roost (a running store) and ran nine miles with her.

Since then we have run together through all that life brings us— through sickness, injury and recovery, good times and hard times. We have laughed and shed tears, side by side. Life is best when shared with others."

Bonding with friends

"I used to run alone. It was my therapy and sometimes my punching bag. But I was stagnant. I met new people and was introduced to new paths and distances when I joined a group. I would never have run my first marathon without their support. The group does more than encourage me to expand my running. These runners have become like family."

"Don't run the New York Marathon without your friend."

"It is okay to share your Body Glide. For every bad thing you say about your husband to your running buddy, you must try to say something good about him."

"I love this group. I read the emails and run when I can. They motivate me even though, because of my schedule, I rarely make it to group runs."

A running friend may, in the end, be more important than a coach.

It's no fun to get muddy without a buddy

Dan Berlin, fourth from left

Seeing the Possibilities

The president of the Fort Collins Running Club was ready to pass on the torch after two years in office. Connie DeMercurio did so knowing that a strong board, bolstered by some enthusiastic new members, would carry on. What she didn't know was that her long-time running partner, Dan Berlin, would step up and agree to lead the running club into the future.

"I was the last man standing," Dan says with a smile. "No one else was ready to take on the job." Dan was happy to take over, delighted, in fact, to pay back the Fort Collins running community for what they have done for him.

At age 43, Dan was struggling with the increasing loss of his sight. Always athletic, he'd been involved with football and track in high school and had frequented the gym regularly in later years. "My longest run in those days was a three-mile jog to the gym," he said.

No longer able to drive or even find his way comfortably around a grocery store, Berlin, owner of a spice business, wanted to find a way to stay fit and release stress. He tried running on a bike path because he could see the edges well enough and traffic was not an issue. It worked. To keep on running, he needed a goal. He set his sights on the 2009 Crossroads Half Marathon in Fort Collins and embarked on a 10-week "intermediate" training program.

Shortly before the race, Dan realized that if he ran solo, he'd be a hazard—to himself and to others in the race. He could not see cones marking the course and running with a crowd of people around him would present a whole new set of problems.

He called Crossroads race director John Lonsdale and asked for help. John sent out an email and in two days Dan had dozens of offers. Connie DeMercurio emerged as the most persistent and got the job. Then began a journey for the pair that over the years has included dozens of races from 5ks to full marathons.

"Let's go," Connie said moments after meeting Dan for the first time.

"There I was in my Crocs, figuring we'd have a bit of conversation before we hit the road, but no, Connie was ready to go the moment she showed up at my house," Dan said. They ran together for two miles that day.

When they race together, an 18-inch nylon cord with a knot at each end tethers them to each other. Connie runs slightly ahead to warn Dan of obstacles. He wears a vest that signals to others that he cannot see.

Dan finished Crossroads in 2 hours, 10 minutes. Goal met. He didn't plan to race again. But then he was invited to be on a relay team participating in the Denver Marathon. "We had a blast," he said. He followed that experience with the Heart Half Marathon in Loveland, a few miles south of Fort Collins. That was the event that hooked him permanently.

In October 2014, Dan ran the rim-to rim-to-rim, a 46-mile jaunt across the Grand Canyon with three friends. "The farthest I'd ever run before that was 27 miles," Dan said. "But I was up for the challenge." He completed the run to enter the history books as the first blind person to accomplish that feat. The whole world took notice.

In 2018, as I write these words, Dan is going strong. His resume now totals 12 marathons, five of them in Boston Marathon, one in New York. In 2013, he stood at the Boston finish line with his then 12-year-old daughter, Talia, as the bomb blast went off half a block away. "I'd finished the race only 15 minutes before, and I wasn't the most coherent, but awesome Talia had her wits about her," Dan said. "She got us back to Cambridge and safely out of the chaos." Later that year, Dan began doing triathlons and in June 2017 he completed the Ironman Triathlon in Boulder, Colorado.

After his rim-to-rim-to-rim experience, Dan joined with Charles Scott, Alison Qualter Berna and Brad Graff, the three-sighted guides who had crossed the Grand Canyon with him, to form Team See Possibilities, a non-profit organization dedicated to supporting children around the world who are blind, and to encourage all people to move beyond their perceived limits.

In 2015, Team Possibilities did the 42k Classic Inca Trail to Machu Picchu, Peru conquering the journey that reached as high at 14,000 feet in 13 hours, traditionally a four-day hike. The following year the team climbed Mount Kilimanjaro in Kenya in two-and-a-half days, trekking at night to highlight the abilities of the blind. Most people take seven days to complete this hike.

In 2017 the team was on the move again, this time to take on an endurance challenge on the Great Wall of China, completing a 100-k run/hike/cycle event. Dan's challenge in the summer of 2018 will be to join an eight-person Team See event to bicycle 3,100 miles across America on tandems with a time limit of nine days.

Dan is a man who has used running and biking to parlay what some would view as a disability into a vehicle to encourage others to make the best of themselves. "It's only an inconvenience," Dan says of his inability to see. He's a humble guy, grateful for what

Still Running

running and the running community has
done for him.

Cindy Valdez

Stories on the Run

Cindy Valdez did her best to get out of running the Rock 'n Roll Half Marathon in Denver in October 2013. She told her husband, Ralph, that she just couldn't do it. She asked her son, Brandon, to take her place. He was busy that day.

So Cindy entered the race, burdened by the sorrow of losing an older sister only a week earlier. "I had no motivation," she said. "But somewhere inside me there was a small voice telling me that I'd trained hard for this race, that I'd paid my money, and that I'd better just do it. The first miles were miserable. I came close to calling Ralph and asking him to come and get me."

Cindy plodded on, with no pressing reason to quit and no real desire to move forward. She's a social person, a true lover of people. By mile nine she needed someone—anyone—to talk to. At her side she caught sight of a young boy, age 14 she learned later, listening to music on his headphones, struggling to keep a decent pace, now and then sinking into a slow shuffle.

"Hi," Cindy said. "How's it going?"

The boy took off his headphones. "This is hard. It's my first half-marathon," came the reply.

"You don't need to take off your headphones," Cindy said.

The boy left his headphones off, wanting to talk. He explained that his parents didn't like it that he'd taken up running. "They say I'm going to ruin my knees, but I love it so much."

"I'm 60 and I've been running for 27 years," Cindy replied. "My knees are just fine."

Then she asked how he had gotten started running. He explained that the year before he'd been in big trouble in school—poor grades, hanging out with a gang of bad kids, and heading down a road to nowhere good. He hinted that he'd spent some time in jail.

After a difficult confrontation with his parents one day, he left the house angry and started to run—as far and as fast as he could. The run made him feel better.

At school he saw a poster inviting kids to join a running club. Before long the boy became dedicated to running. He came to see it as the thing that had turned his life around.

As Cindy listened to his story, the miles clicked away for both of them. She knew now she'd finish the Rock 'n Roll Half Marathon.

The boy's pace slowed and Cindy stayed at his side, planning to finish with him. He encouraged her to go ahead and finally she did, sensitive to the fact that he needed his music to keep him going and that he would probably feel most comfortable completing this challenge alone.

Cindy searched for the boy at the finish line, but didn't find him among the crowds of people. "I'm sure he finished," she said. "No doubt about it."

Her story was finished now, and so was the ten-mile training run Cindy and I had completed side-by-side on a stunning Saturday morning in the foothills near our home.

Life is story and sharing stories with each other enhances friendship. Long runs give us the gift of time to listen

Choosing What to Eat

Anyone who has been running for a while has developed some strong opinions about the food they eat and when they eat it, before and after training runs and races. By trial and error they have learned what works best for them. Not surprisingly, given the way attitudes and theories on most any subject have a way of changing over time, "professional" notions of how and what runners should eat have run the gamut over the years.

I remember reading a *Runner's World* article, "Running on Empty" suggesting that the best way to approach even a very long race, was with an empty stomach. There have been coffee advocates insisting that a jolt of caffeine is helpful prior to a race. I remember reading about a top Ironman competitor who fueled up by eating a dozen potatoes.

Carbo-loading prior to a race has long been touted as the best way to prepare for a long race. Many races sponsor spaghetti dinners the night before an event and there's usually a meat and non-meat version of the accompanying sauce. Complex carbohydrates provide slow and steady fuel for long runs. A pre-race meal should go easy on fat, which takes a long time to digest, and fiber that can cause bloating and intestinal problems during a long period of exertion. One runner says she'll eat "anything but eel" before a race but insists on the importance of a glass of wine. My choice is a whole box of macaroni and cheese. It's not for everyone!

Runners burn about 100 calories per mile and to function most efficiently in action, their muscles need extra protein. Good sources are eggs, nuts, fish, chicken and tofu. The healthiest fats are found in olive, flaxseed and canola oil and avocados. Eight cups of liquid consumed evenly during the day before a long run or race is recommended. Water is the number one choice but other liquids, as long as they are not dehydrating like coffee and soda, count.

Quirks and superstitions around eating prior to and after a race are common. Early on race morning, my choice is half a bagel with peanut butter. During a race I drink three small gulps of water at every aid station and at mile eight of a half-marathon I suck on a gel cube.

On race morning, runners choose from oatmeal with milk and dried fruit, bananas, energy bars, a waffle with syrup or a bowl of rice. For some, toast or a bagel with peanut butter works well. Smoothies, fruit juice and sports drinks are popular and help with hydration. It's important not to eat anything new and different before a race, and to drink plenty of water along with whatever you eat. Practice a pre-race eating routine and discover what works best for you.

After a race, refuel within 30 minutes as the body utilizes nourishment most efficiently during this window of time. At the end of an event you'll find everything from beer to burritos, barbecue to bananas. In moderation, go with whatever looks best to you. One runner told me that she likes to eat a big bowl of tapioca after a long run.

The expression, *You are what you eat,* rings true. Also true: *Variety is the spice of life.*

Jeni Arndt and Libby James

The End of an Era

2014: "The end of an era," my 49-year-old daughter, Jeni, said with a smile, turning her head to address me as she approached from behind. We were on top of a hill less than halfway through a snowy Horsetooth Half Marathon in the foothills of Northern Colorado in April. "I'm sticking with you until the finish," she announced.

I didn't say anything. That was because I couldn't. I was busy breathing. We ran side-by-side for a while. I was concentrating hard on just maintaining my pace. My feelings were mixed. It was high time my youngest kid beat me in a half-marathon. She had outraced me once in a 5k, then promptly threw up at the finish line and vowed never to do *that* again. So here she is, at it again.

I wanted her to beat me. I really did. At least most of me did. I was okay with ending an era. Every era must end, right? But I was not going to give up on this one for free. She'd have to earn it fair and square.

I have several grandsons who have not considered me any sort of competition for several years now, as well they should not. Granddaughters? One can beat me. The others are working on it.

Kristin, my older daughter, has it figured out. She runs regularly and well and has done so for many years. She loves marathons and has done more than a dozen, including braving the challenge of New York. She's dedicated to the sport and at the same time, does not have a competitive bone in her body—at least when it comes to running. (She's an attorney with a demanding career.) She was never any good at selling candy when she was a Camp Fire Girl, either. Being the one who sold the most meant nothing to her. In her running life, she takes pleasure in the journey, in the tight relationship she has with her best running buddy, and in the way running makes her feel and look and approach life. She runs at her own pace, without giving a thought to any possible competition.

After a while, the snow falling in the foothills didn't quit but small blessing, it quit blasting Jeni and me in the face. My daughter, in her moth-eaten, brown, recycled, cashmere sweater and no gloves, seemed more than elated with what she was doing. After another plodding mile or so, she disappeared from view.

The first two miles of HTH are such an uphill grind that exhaustion sets in early. The later and somewhat less intimidating hills provide diversion, but the last few flat miles on the bike path into the finish at New Belgian Brewery near downtown Fort Collins, seem to go on forever and have always been the toughest part of the course for me. There are no obstacles to divert one's attention from the fact that 13 miles is a long way to run and getting longer with every year for me. And so I plodded on, more a mind game than a leg game at this point.

I didn't see Jeni at the finish line. I knew she had a plane to catch and would dash for home the minute the race was over. Soggy and cold, I hung around at the finish, greeting friends and wondering where she was.

I didn't have long to wait. She was hard to miss in that stylish outfit and only three minutes behind me. Fast enough for third in her age group. The good news is, at age 49, she was about to "age up" to the 50-54 age group.

When she was 53, Jeni caught up with me again during a downhill half marathon, insisting she did that to encourage me to speed up as the finish line approached. I did.

I'm still waiting for her to beat me.

Awards on the shelf

Honoring Awards

Some people have been running for years but have never entered a race Maybe that's a good thing. It means you don't have a pile of heavy medals complete with big, wide ribbons that you wore proudly for 10 to 30 minutes after a race but haven't figured out what to do with them since you took them off. Have you ever seen anyone wearing a finishing medal at any time other than right after a race?

If you find yourself in the winners' circle, you might have more than a few medals to settle into a permanent home. Awards come in all shapes and sizes and every single one is appreciated. But that doesn't mean that they aren't a problem at times.

A local potter and also a runner, T.S. Berger, has made the awards for the Fourth of July race in Fort Collins for longer than I can remember. They're useful items—everything from platters and bowls to canisters and containers of all sorts. I love them and use them all.

Over time, I've won everything from a genuine simulated walnut toilet seat to a Kokopelli figure mounted on a rock. (I have two of these.) I have a lifetime supply of trivets, tiles and plaques, a moveable action figure, and a set of tinkling bells, all different sizes, from long-ago Bonne Bell women's races.

I also have two tiny silver charms on a bracelet from Freihofer's women's 5k race in Albany, New York. They are my idea of the perfect award: small, beautiful and wearable.

I treasure every item but I struggle with housing them. My home is small and I feel a little uncomfortable featuring running trophies front and center. Most of them are packed into a bookcase in my dining room.

A series of circumstances, mostly related to my ancient age, found me the recipient of not one but two enormous cups on a heavy stand after competing in two Doubles races. What do to with them?

I moved one of the cups into a corner of my bathroom where it holds bars of soap. It's visible, at least to anyone in my house who uses the facilities, and it serves a purpose. The other one I sent home with a runner friend who coveted it.

What do other runners do with their medals? One I know tried removing the ribbons and hanging the medals on her

Christmas tree. Only a temporary use and they were so heavy that they caused the tree branches to droop. Another has a bathroom devoted to displaying running awards. Still another has a family room with a large wooden beam that has plenty of space for displaying awards.

The Flying Pig race in Fort Collins gets the prize for an award that is both unique and useful. It is a tiny compressed package, about three by five inches that when soaked in water, grows into 100-percent cotton, bright pink boxer shorts with flying pigs all over them. My package was marked with an "L" which stood for large. I had to improvise a way to keep them in place. Races used to award running shoes to winners. Those were the best awards ever. If shoes are not an option, I'd like to suggest awards that are modest, practical and don't take up too much space.

40-44 Jennifer Rhines 15:58 45-49 Leslee Hoey 19:54 50-54 Marisa Sutera Strange 18:32 55-59 Nancy Stewart 19:38

60-64 Coreen Steinbach 21:38 65-69 Sabra Harvey 20:27 70-74 Jan Holmquist 22:16 75-79 Libby James 24:00

80-84 Anny Stockman 35:46

**2014 Syracuse Festival
Women's Age Group Winners**

USATF National 5K Master's Championships

rhbrockj11@me.com

Running Late

"It's an exciting, cutting-edge field with discoveries in science and performances showing the best is still ahead."

The above is a direct quote from Dr. Cathy Utzschneider referring to recent research on masters athletes (those over 40). A professor of physiology and competitive performance at Boston College, Utzschneider's ground-breaking book, *Mastering Running* is the culmination of knowledge gained during seven years' of doctoral study and her personal experience as a competitive athlete and coach for Liberty Athletic Club in Boston with members ranging from their 20s to 70s.

Also author of *MOVE!,* promoting the benefits of exercise, Cathy is a regular contributor to *National Masters Running News.* "You want to keep training when you know that exercise can increase the size of your brain's frontal lobes controlling decision-making, multitasking, learning and memory," Cathy says.

She didn't run seriously until after the birth of her first child when she was forty, yet has racked up seven national masters track/cross country championships, a number five in the world age group ranking, and an indoor national 3k championship for women age 55.

On the national scene, evidence that older runners are thriving and maintaining speed ranges from facts like Colorado's Colleen DeRueck qualifying for the 2016 Olympic Marathon trials at age 49, Kathy Martin's 40:10 10k at the USATF National Masters Championships at age 62, an American record, not to mention 95-year-old Olga Kotelko's record as a track champion.

At age 91, Harriette Thompson of North Carolina completed the San Diego Rock and Roll Marathon in a record time of 7:07:42, then went home to celebrate with Sydnor, her husband of 67 years. "I feel wonderful," she said. "I feel very relieved and I feel very anxious to take a shower and then fall into bed. "If I'm around, I'll be back next year," she promised. Any way you cut it, seven hours is a long time to spend on your feet, however old you are and whatever you are doing.

In 2017 at age 94, Harriette walked and jogged the Rock 'n Roll Half Marathon in San Diego. She died a few months later, the result of a fall she took while delivering a birthday gift to a friend.

And isn't that what it's all about: Keeping on keeping on, not because you're going to get faster but because you love what you're doing and you want to do it as long as you can. My guess is that unless you're passionate about putting one foot in front of the other, you're not likely to keep it up over time just because it's good for you.

Older runners may have more fun. Giving up a few seconds or minutes to Old Father Time doesn't bother oldsters as long as they can stay in the game. In the words of former *Runners World* editor Amby Burfoot, "...there is no failure in running, or in life, as long as you keep moving."

Bill Watts, author of *Running for the Average Joe,* has a favorite quote also. "The worst thing about running is not running."

Mastering Running and *Running for the Average Joe* are available online at Amazon and in local bookstores.

Ouch!

Injury: A Good Reminder

It's Friday and I just got back from a fantastic, memorable, totally wonderful, extremely slow, early morning run. I didn't take a watch. I don't know how fast or how far I went. My experience was noticeably different from my usual self-prescribed run of a somewhat set pace and distance. I'm icing my left calf as I write this.

It has been a long time since I've been injured, but last week-end I had to gimp home more than two miles from a planned six-mile run because the muscle in my left calf was screaming. I had no idea what might be causing the pain.

On Monday I didn't run. *Time for a break,* I told myself, though honestly, I had no choice. I iced my calf muscle several times during the day. By Tuesday, I could walk a mile without much pain. On Friday I ran that slow and pleasurable run of around three miles. With every step, I was aware of my sore muscle, but it became less noticeable as the minutes ticked by, letting me know that I probably wasn't doing any further damage. My calf was letting me run.

I finished these few miles with sincere appreciation, reminded once again of the amazing healing ability of the human body. I realized that I needed to respect my body more than I do. I used to be an avid and consistent stretcher before I went for a run. Then pre-run stretching went out of style, and I wasn't going to argue with that. These days I do a random few stretches at no particular time, and at least once a week I do a Pilates workout. Maybe not enough, I think.

I have learned through experience that the more I run, the tighter my muscles become. And then one day those muscles say, *Whoa! Tend to me.* It is so easy to forget. After this wake-up call, I'm planning to do some stretching every time before I run and then stretch some more afterwards. And I'm contemplating some cross-training. My bicycle is in sad need of a workout, and a hike in the hills is calling.

Danger lurks, I know. It is too easy to fall back into old patterns. Running has the allure of being so accessible. Just throw on a pair of shoes and step out the door. And so efficient—40 minutes and you have completed a workout. It is a good thing to mix it up. Take the time to drive to a special trailhead, lace up the hiking boots and soak up the scenery. Or pump up those bicycle tires and go for a ride.

As my mistreated muscle began to heal, I enjoyed running slowly, with no thoughts of how fast or how far and taking the time to appreciate the fact that I am able to run at all.

The Great Equalizer

"Are runners different from other athletes?" I asked this question of a running friend as we set out early on a Sunday morning. A good bit of chatter and a couple of miles later, we decided that perhaps they are.

The week before we'd experienced two Fort Collins traditions, the Mountain Avenue Mile and the Run for Hope 5k. Both these events reflected special caring as they contributed to local non-profits and offered opportunities for happy interaction.

"In what other sport," my friend asked, "do the top athletes regularly compete with the middle-of-the-road and back-of-the-pack competitors?" I wonder if LeBron James has pick-up games with local high school basketball players on his off-days. I doubt it. I'm betting he doesn't shoot baskets with the guys on the corner who need to stop to catch their breath after every shot.

My friend chatted on, as I became quiet, struggling to keep up. "Every weekend top runners line up at hundreds of running events across the country, to compete with weekend warriors and the run-walk-run crowd pushing strollers and tugging or being tugged by their dogs. Every time, you'll see the winners warming down along the last yards of the course, cheering on their co-runners as they make their way to the finish line. And when the race is over, participants don't hurry home. Instead they hang around rehydrating, snacking and re-living the race with friends and strangers alike."

We asked ourselves what it was that caused these people to bond. Is it that everyone who runs understands the effort involved, no matter what the pace? When you run as fast as you can, the degree of effort is similar, regardless of the end result.

My friend recalled a time during the Colorado Run 10k race when the course finished by circling a long oval drive on the Colorado State University campus. As he approached the last half-mile or so, my friend came upon an unlikely-looking woman participant muttering to herself, "Come on legs, come on legs."

"My respect for this lady was growing, but I was not going to let her beat me," he said. "At the finish, barely ahead of her and gasping for air, I watched as she joined friends in animated conversation. That was the moment when I began to appreciate running as a great equalizer. That conclusion has been reinforced for me many times over."

The talented few who make running really fast look effortless are often genetically blessed freaks of nature. Yet, they are human and need to train, eat with care and deal with injuries as every runner must. Many of them embrace the camaraderie among runners along with everyone else in the race.

Awards are given by age and gender as a way to give every participant a fair chance at mounting the podium to receive an award.

The nature of what runners do, more than often not, creates within them a connection with other runners that is rare in most other sports. Even the best runners recognize and honor the effort that must be expended by any runner determined to do his or her best.

Regardless of talent and skill, runners love to cheer each other on. Those infected with the running bug have a mutual understanding and a relationship with each other that I think is unique.

Green Events race directors, Ron Baker and
Lisa Sinclair

Behind the Scenes: The Life of Race Directors

I've been in awe of race directors for a long
time now. I can't imagine being able to do all
that they do in order to pull off a successful
running race. Large race or small, there are
always a zillion details that must be attended
to from making sure there are enough porta-
potties to rounding-up and counting on
volunteers, arranging for T-shirts, medals
and awards, making sure the course is
measured, traffic is controlled and aid

stations are manned and supplied. Much of what they do is not obvious to those of us who participate in racing events—unless of course—something goes wrong.

Lisa Sinclair and Ron Baker of Green Events and I sat soaking up the autumn sun outside a café in downtown Fort Collins one afternoon and talked about what it's like to be a full-time race director.

In 2011, Ron, a recently retired dentist, who'd been running for nearly 30 years, met Lisa when they shared the same running coach and discovered that they had compatible ideas about environmental and social sustainability.

Ron was looking for a second career and Lisa, who had been working for a local health club, was ready to put her extensive education and experience in sports science, physiology and business into practice in an endeavor of her own.

Green Events was born. Today Lisa and Ron own and sponsor many events every year beginning with the Sweaty Sweater 5k and Polar Plunge into icy Horsetooth Reservoir in the foothills west of Fort Collins in January and ending with the Equinox Half Marathon in September, also in the foothills. (They camped out overnight near the finish line before that one the first time they directed it.) They also manage a number of fundraising running events for non-profit organizations.

Their passion for preserving the environment and contributing a portion of

race proceeds to non-profits is as important
to them as is their commitment to running.
In 2010, when they worked together in a
zero-waste effort for the Colorado Marathon
and the Horsetooth Half in Fort Collins, they
achieved a whopping 90% of race-related
materials recycled.

The hardest thing about their job is the
pressure that builds close to race time to
make sure they've tended to every detail.
Despite the sleep deprivation, they derive
great satisfaction from creating a race that
runs smoothly and provides a memorable
experience for the participants.

"The flurry of emails I have to deal with is
one of the hardest parts of my job," Lisa said.
Sometimes she forwards them to Ron for a
laugh. The week before a recent event, a race
entrant emailed to ask if Lisa could either
find her a babysitter or change the starting
time of the race for her convenience.

Runners love T-shirts and they're
passionate about medals, Ron has learned.
After failing to offer a finishing medal for the
inaugural running of their the Equinox Fall
Half Marathon, he caved in. Ron had felt that
medals made in China weren't a good fit for a
green event. When Lisa found a Colorado
source using recycled materials, the problem
was solved and runners went home happy
with their medals the next year.

Behind-the-scenes race planning begins as
long as a year before an event and continues
until the last bin of recycled trash is hauled

away. And in between there are those endless details.

Green Events is growing. In 2017 the company directed 21 events including a Spring Equinox Half Marathon, 10k race, and Fourth of July 5k that drew close to 1,000 entrants and featured an elite division with prize money. Total Green Events participants for 2017 reached 6,800. The organization sponsored a scholarship for a high school student, achieved a recycling rate of 95 percent at their events and donated more than $27,000 to non-profits—a dive rescue team, high school cross-country teams, and an organization dedicated to preserving the integrity of the Poudre River that flows through Fort Collins.

Lisa and Ron agree. They couldn't do it without dedicated volunteers. And they wouldn't trade their jobs for anything.

Thank goodness for people like Lisa and Ron who are committed to seeing that running races are positive experiences for every entrant, take an active role in preserving the environment and stay committed to following their dream.

Gavin, Jamie, Patrick, and Grady Arnold

Thinking about Having a Baby?

Jamie Schiel Arnold has been running for as long as she can remember, often to stay in shape for other sports. When offered college scholarships in cross country, basketball and soccer, she chose cross country and participated in division one cross country and track teams for four years. She qualified for the Boston Marathon in her first race at that distance in 2006 and won the Water to Wine Half Marathon in Sonoma, California in 2013.

She married at age 26 and works as a project engineer at Ball Aerospace in Boulder, Colorado. Jamie always knew she wanted a family. At age 30, after a summer of hard training and "pre-baby fun," she and her husband agreed that they were ready. Their son Gavin was born in October 2014.

During the first four months of her pregnancy, Jamie ran comfortably, keeping her heart rate under 140 bpm. "During months five and six it got harder," she said. "I felt I needed to keep running to stay sane, but eventually my body told me it was time to stop." She began taking long daily walks.

While her running friends swear that running made their deliveries easier, Jamie isn't sure she agrees. "I don't know but I think that running helped with focus and getting down to business," she said.

Two days after Jamie came home from the hospital, she began walking. With her son Gavin strapped into a front pack, she gradually added time to her walks and within a week was up to an hour. After five weeks she did her first post-partum run, one-fourth-mile run/walk intervals for three miles, a regime she adjusted as she became stronger. Her workouts were on a treadmill unless her husband was home and she could run outside, a welcome alone time for her.

Her job allowed her a twelve-week maternity leave before she began a balancing act: incorporating parenting, work and running. She began to run at noon when work permitted. "When I got home, I wanted to spend as much time as possible with my little dude," she said.

She says that there's advice about running while pregnant but not much about getting back into shape after delivery. She did take note of one runner's blog that suggested exercises to strengthen the pelvic floor and wearing pads under your running bra and black shorts or tights. Otherwise, she's been on her own to get back into her former running shape.

Her advice is to keep your sessions, whether running or walking, enjoyable. "Don't overdo it and get hurt."

In December 2017, Gavin became big brother to Patrick. Even though she was able to take another twelve-week maternity leave from her job at Ball Aerospace, Jamie elected to keep Gavin's daycare routine the same as when she was working full-time. This allowed her lots of quality time with Patrick during his first months of life.

Back at work and back to running, she is looking forward to a half-marathon this fall in Cheyenne, the town where she grew up. "I like having a goal," Jamie said. "I need to have something to satisfy my competitive nature."

Along with several family members, there will be two small boys among her cheering section at the race.

"I'm loving it," she says of parenthood. "There's nothing like it."

Joe Friel

The Big Five O Need not Slow you Down— Much

One day, more than three decades ago, my son Jeff came home from Rocky Mountain High School in Fort Collins to report that his history teacher was planning to run in the Denver Marathon that spring. So was I. That was when I was first introduced to Joe Friel.

Fast After Fifty: how to race strong for the rest of your life, is Joe's twelfth book about athletic training and it's a winner. I was touched by his hand-written note when he sent me a copy recalling the longevity of our friendship and the fact that it mattered to him.

What's a history teacher doing writing nationally acclaimed books about the technicalities of training for sport? Turns out Joe is over-the-top qualified. He holds a masters degree in exercise science and before he developed a reputation as an elite triathlon and cycling coach, he owned Foot of the Rockies in Fort Collins, likely the first triathlon store in the world. During 30 years of coaching, he has trained national and world championship athletes such as Olympian Ryan Bolton, winner of the 2002 Ironman Triathlon in Lake Placid.

As his experience and expertise grew, Joe began to write about endurance sports. Among his sixteen books as of 2017, are the best-selling *Training Bible* series for triathletes, cyclists and mountain bikers. He has been featured in *Bicycling, Outside, Runners' World, Triathlete, VeloNews* and many other magazines.

This guy never stops. In 1999 he co-founded with his son Dirk, an accomplished cyclist, TrainingPeaks.com. that has become the leading provider of training software for endurance athletes around the world. Joe presents at athlete seminars and coaching conferences, offers training camps for athletes, and frequently consults with the sports equipment industry.

In his own right as an athlete, Joe has been a Colorado State Masters Triathlon champion, a perennial All-American age group athlete and a USATF-regional multisport champion.

He describes *Fast After Fifty* as a present to himself on the occasion of his seventieth birthday. "I was afraid of rapidly deceasing athletic performance," he admits. "I decided to read all the research I could find on aging and endurance." He began by posting blogs on the subject on joefrielsblog.com. They were so well received that he knew he had to write a book about what he was learning.

The result covers myths about aging, how normal aging differs from athletic aging, how exercise affects us as we age, the roles of nature and nurture and what we can do to slow or even temporarily reverse changes that occur. He makes specific and concrete suggestions about training routines, recovery, sleep, diet and nutrition. All his statements are backed up by meticulous research.

The best thing about *Fast After Fifty* is that it's fun to read. Joe's personality comes through on every page. He's done his homework. He's a techie kind of guy who loves delving into research. He pulls no punches, acknowledging that there are still areas where the answers are not cut and dried and will differ with the passage of time as more and more athletes move into older age groups. "Everyone is different," he says, asserting that the volume and intensity of training regimes and diet must be tailored to the individual. In this business one size does not fit all.

Readers don't learn about Joe's personal vulnerability and why he's working harder than ever to take his own advice until near the end of his book. These days he and his wife Joyce, train on their bicycles nearly year-

round in Arizona. They return to Colorado for
a couple of months every summer.

Libby James

Annoying strap syndrome

Encumbered Running

In early May one year, a young woman from
the *Boulder Daily Camera* newspaper
contacted me and conducted a brief phone
interview about my long-time participation
in the Bolder Boulder 10k held on Memorial
Day each spring. The event marks the start of
the summer running season in these parts,
and attracts as many as 50,000 runners from
all over the world.

The journalist and I had a pleasant visit and
then she asked about a photo. I offered to
send her one but she said the paper would

send a photographer to my house. I was a
little surprised as I live 50-plus miles from
Boulder.

We set a date for the photographer to
arrive at 7:30 a.m. one morning. I was to run
my normal route and the photographer
would follow me and snap pictures.

I decided in honor of the upcoming race, to
wear my new Bolder Boulder age-group
champion shirt earned at the most recent
running of the Bolder Boulder last May. It
was a little small and not too comfortable. It
looked pretty bad when worn without a bra.
But I never wear a bra when I run.

The day before the planned photo shoot, I
learned that Go Lite, a company that made
great sports clothing, was having a
warehouse clearance sale. My 16-year-old
granddaughter and I decided to check it out.
We had a fun time looking through the racks
of shirts and pants and stacks of underwear.
She chose a sturdy running bra. Hmm, I
thought. Maybe I should shape up and get
myself one of those.

I tried one on. It was tight—they all are.
They're supposed to be. That's why I don't
like to wear them. *Okay. Get over it,* I told
myself. I bought the bra.

The next morning I strapped on my new
bra before I slipped the Bolder Boulder shirt
over my head. After I did this, I began to
wonder if I was going to be able to run in this
already uncomfortable get-up.

I got a little nervous waiting for the
photographer to arrive. I stepped outside my

front door and swept the porch. The photographer fellow showed up on time and seemed friendly enough.

He asked me to start my run. He jumped into his car and was soon ahead of me. He popped up a few blocks down the road and started snapping away. Then he jumped back into his car and moved ahead. This routine continued for almost four miles. Now and then I made some inane comment as I tried to make myself look, well, good, and like a runner. The photographer kept on hopping in and out of his car and snapping away. Once he emerged from behind a bush and surprised me.

Back at my house, he came inside and shot me taking off my shoes, then in my living room surrounded by old running shoes, and finally wandering around in my back garden. By the time he finished, he'd shot more than 600 photos and my smile muscles were suffering from exhaustion and in worse shape than my legs.

The first thing I did after the photographer waved goodbye was to hustle into my bedroom take off that blasted bra. Then I took a deep breath.

Along with the story, a single photo appeared in the *Boulder Camera* article.

Age-graded cup from Doubles Road Race

The Older the Better

Have you heard? Time takes its toll. There's
no arguing with the fact that runners peak at
a certain age. No one can peg exactly when.
Several factors are involved: genes, fitness
level, the number of years one has been
running and training regularly, nutrition,
gender, and state of mind.

Runners between the ages of 19 and 29 are
generally at the top of their game. If they are

ever going to win a race, chances are they will do it when they are somewhere between these ages. (The possible exception is the full marathon when runners tend to peak at a slightly older age.)

I have heard it said that runners can expect to improve their times for seven years after they begin regular training. But if you start when you are 65, it is likely to be tough, but perhaps not impossible, to improve for seven years.

The speed at which they run matters not a whit to many runners, arguably the wisest ones. Yet there are plenty of runners of all ages in search of ways to cut a few seconds off their 5k or 10k times as they chase after a "PR," (a personal record).

In order to level the playing field for runners of all ages, an age-graded scale came into being in 2002 and has been gaining in visibility and credibility ever since. The scale has been revised and adjusted twice, in 2010 and in 2015 to account for faster times among older runners.

I must have had my head in the sand because I had never heard of the age-graded scale when I went to Seattle in 2011 to participate in the National Cross Country Club Championships. The event was new to me in lots of ways. It took place on a golf course. I'd never run cross-country before and dutifully inserted spikes into my racing flats—and after the race I couldn't get them out again.

I learned that the age-graded score serves as a handicap arrived at by taking into account a competitor's age and time. Tables are compiled by the world governing body for masters track and field, long distance running and race walking.

Scores are given in percentages. Some running statisticians believe age-grade scoring is the fairest way to acknowledge the accomplishments of all race participants.

Oh yes. Time brings with it change. Age-graded scores are a fine way to keep oldsters competing, level the playing field, encourage oldsters to continue competing and to allow runners to look forward to their birthdays.

Penny Tisko demonstrates the Pose Method

A New Way to Run

It was serendipitous, the way I learned about the Pose Method of running. I'd never heard of Dr. Nicholas Romanoff, who'd been espousing a way to run faster, more efficiently and more injury-free for several decades. Penny Tisko, an elite masters runner who'd been plagued with injuries for eight years, told me her story over lunch one day before a race in Albany, New York when we happened to land at the same table.

"For a long time, I had been searching for a better way to run and not get injured," Tisko said, pointing out that 82 % of runners experience frequent injuries. She found the answer she sought in the Pose Method.

After a period of dedicated effort learning and implementing the Pose Method, Tisko explained her admiration for Romanoff, calling him "a brilliant and kind man." She described her journey toward certification as a Pose Method instructor, and her anticipated return to racing, something she once thought she'd never be able to do again.

It wasn't until a second meeting with Tisko when she generously shared some of the basics of the method, that I became truly intrigued. "Running is a skill," she said. "Like any other sport, it takes practice to run efficiently and well."

This is a philosophy that emerged following publication of Christopher McDougall's book, *Born to Run.* Natural Running, Chi Running and Evolution Running are movements that have also become popular since then.

Dr. Romanoff, a Ph.D sports scientist and coach in the Soviet Union athletic system during the 1970s, used physics to figure out the elements that made for the best way to run. In a book, *Power, Speed, Endurance: A Skill-Based Approach to Endurance Training,* Brian MacKenzie describes Romanoff's method as "using gravity to fall forward and shifting support by dropping the feet directly under the body as you move forward. Gravity is the one relentless force that influences all in terms of movement, and to run well your best bet is to use gravity as best you can as opposed to fighting it," MacKenzie writes.

Learning how to fall is the most essential step in adopting the Pose Technique, according to Valerie Hunt, a coach and runner who improved her mile pace by more than a minute and a half using the method. "It's scary," she said. "Your body will fight you on it at first by naturally breaking the fall. You have to practice until your brain gets the message that this falling thing is something you really want to do."

Tisko emphasizes the "free energy" derived from practicing the method. At a mini-clinic she conducted, she explained that there was a great deal to learn about the technique including the importance of maintaining a cadence of 180 beats per minute, concentrating on using gravitational force rather than muscular effort, and avoiding heel strike in favor of landing on the forefoot. She recommends lightweight flexible shoes as a way to avoid heel striking and overstriding. "We can all improve if we are willing to work on our technique," she promises.

A ten-lesson program is detailed in *The Running Revolution: How to Run Faster, Farther and Injury-Free for Life* by Dr. Nicholas Romanoff and Kurt Brungardt published by Penguin Books in 2014. It's surprising what some simple adjustments can make to running efficiency.

Bikes meet tractors in the farmland

Bikers Explore Colorado Agriculture

Almost everyone who lives in or and close to Colorado knows about Ride the Rockies, a week-long bicycle tour in the high country that has been around since the '80s. You have to be lucky in the lottery to get into that ride these days.

Not so with Pedal the Plains, a three-day bike tour in the high plains of eastern Colorado where fewer than 800 riders completed the fourth annual ride in 2014.

As a five-time survivor of RAGBRAI, the ride across Iowa that attracts as many as 20,000 cyclists, I was so happy to be part of a so much smaller group in Colorado. No one waited more that a few moments to use a porta potty or get a meal, there were plenty of spaces to put up a tent, and you didn't take your life in your hands because of heavy two-wheeled traffic to mount your bike or stop along the road.

Pedal the Plains is special because it goes through the vast agricultural countryside that is the eastern third of Colorado. It is set up to include "educational" stops at historic farms, museums in tiny towns, car collections and shows and displays of everything from wind power to enormous farm machinery.

And all along the way, there are informative signs explaining what Colorado produces, how it rates among other states and its various claims to agricultural fame. I now know that there are more than 36,000 farms and ranches in the state with an average size of 881 acres. And I'd know a whole lot more if I could read faster or pedal more slowly as the signs showed up on the side of the road.

The ride is billed as "a celebration of Colorado's cycling culture" and is put on by the *Denver Post* and the state of Colorado. Proceeds benefit the communities that host the event, and the *Denver Post* Community Foundation to support Future Farmers of America and Colorado 4-H.

I rode with my younger daughter. We've done a good bit of biking together over the years, but none recently. It was like old times loading bikes a bit haphazardly onto the car, setting up our tent at the end of the day, enduring a few freezing moments in the morning and spending the whole day outdoors, riding, soaking up the sun, confronting the wind, a nearly constant visitor to the plains, and chatting with strangers and friends on the road. It was great to be out there!

The ride is held the third week of September every year and the route varies, always including three eastern Colorado communities. This year we began in Julesburg, population 1,225, rode to Holyoke, with 2,300 residents, then to Sterling, the largest town on the plains with more than 14,000 souls, and back to Julesburg on the final day, pausing just across the border into Nebraska long enough to take a photo to prove that we were there. The host communities benefit from an explosion of people for a few short hours. The chosen towns are a well-kept secret until registration opens for the ride every year.

I'm a fan. Wherever the ride is going in the future, I'll be back.

Flying Pig award winners showing off their prizes

The Flying Pig Gig

Pigs took to the air for the eighth annual Flying Pig 5k Run/Walk at 8:30 a.m. on April 10, 2016 at Spring Canyon Park, 2626 Horsetooth Road. Did you know that an expression like "when pigs fly" is called an adnayton-- a way of saying something that will never happen. "When Hell freezes over," is another common adnayton.

In addition to benefitting a great cause— the Foothills Gateway Family Support Services Program—The Flying Pig Run is a terrific race for lots of reasons.

The course winds around Spring Canyon Park, on broad paths, some pavement and some dirt. It's flat and it is almost certain that there will be at least a spring breeze—

and sometimes more--to assist or challenge runners depending on the direction they are headed.

The entrance fee is a modest $25, $30 on race day and includes a T-shirt and a bacon bagel breakfast. There's a 10% discount for teams of four or more.

The course is certified and is a qualifying race for the Bolder Boulder on Memorial Day. In that huge 10k race, runners are divided into waves according to prior race times they submit when they sign up.

The Flying Pig race includes a Piglet Walk, free for kids 10 and under. Each little piglet walker gets a treat at the finish.

Awards are most unusual: Neat little packages, about three inches square that, when submerged in water, morph into bright pink boxer shorts with flying pigs all over them. They are worth running your heart out for.

"We staged the first ever Flying Pigs Run in a blizzard," race director Pam Miller remembered. "Seventy people showed up. We had a few cones to mark the course and someone to shovel the snow." The race wasn't even timed that year but within a couple of years numbers had grown to 475 and the finish had become much more official.

Pam has been with Foothills Gateway, an organization that serves people with disabilities in the community, for more than three decades, serving as children's case manager there. She likes her job so much that she expects her boss to find her "fossilized over her desk" one day.

"The race grew out of a fundraiser that Pam dreamed up. She organized a team to place flying pig yard signs in the homes of likely donors and then charged them to have the signs removed. "It got a little labor intensive," Pam said. "That's when we decided to do a race instead."

She explained that funds raised go to assist families who have disabled children living at home, to purchase assistive devices, to sponsor "respitality" times when children can go to Respite Care free of charge, and to host free movie-and-pizza nights for families. "The funds raised by the race allow us to help with extra things that parents find difficult to afford," Pam said. "We have a whole lot of fun in the process."

Still Running

Sunset on the road, Wild West Relay

Memorable Runs

What makes a run one you'll recall weeks, months, even years hence, that will continue to inspire you, make you feel grateful, joyous, thoughtful, introspective or soothe a hurt? Sometimes it is because of a realization, the celebration of a meaningful event, or because the run was in a place that held special meaning.

A few of the friends I run with shared their most memorable runs.

"When my dad died, I arrived home from

my Peace Corps assignment in Morocco,
tired, stressed, and jetlagged. I couldn't sleep,
so I got up at 4:00 a.m. and went for a run. I
remember thinking that running had saved
my life--several times by now. I was back
home by 6:30 a. m. My brother was up. 'Hey,
wanna go for a run?' he asked.

"Too late, I already ran 16," I said. "That
run got me through the day of my dad's
memorial service."

"I keep going back to this run I had long
ago. It was simply out my front door after
work, at dusk, onto the Highline Canal in
Denver, my normal route. My kids were little
so I was happy to have a moment to myself. I
wasn't planning to run more than four
miles. It was snowing lightly, with a little
accumulation, quiet in that way that the
falling snow makes things. I remember
thinking, *This is just so nice and peaceful.* I still
have this memory of such a pleasant, relaxing
run, perhaps because usually snow is more a
pain in the neck than peaceful. That run has
stuck with me for 20 years."

"Tokyo! My first and last marathon on the
occasion of my 65th birthday, high fiving with
volunteers along the way, partaking in wine
and beer stops en route, but skipping the
mystery foods as I headed for a slow and
comfortable five-hour finish time. Most
challenging was finding friends at the end
among 36,000 runners before indulging in a
hot water soak and a celebratory margarita."

"At a half marathon in Hawaii, as Frank
Shorter presented my award, I mentioned

that I was from Colorado, where he lives. We chatted for a moment and then he gave me a hug and kissed my cheek. For the rest of the day, I kept saying, 'Wow. I got kissed by Frank Shorter.' At a recent half marathon in Massachusetts, I met and talked with Bill Rodgers. No kiss this time but I got his autograph on my race bib. He wrote, 'Let's run forever.'"

"The sheer joy of realizing I could run again following hip surgery overwhelmed me on my first time out the door. I paused for a light to turn green and began to sob uncontrollably. As I crossed the street, a lady on the other side asked if I was all right. It was my pleasure to assure her that I was."

"I ran the Marine Corps Marathon with my son when he was recovering from an injury and spending long hours at work. This meant that I could actually keep up with him! We talked the entire way and at the end I was stronger and "carried" him through the last six miles. That day I became his running buddy rather than his aging mother. We crossed the finish line holding hands and he choked up at the end. It was my best run ever."

There is no way to orchestrate the run that will become an especially memorable one, but we can all learn to recognize and appreciate it when that special run comes our way.

Libby James

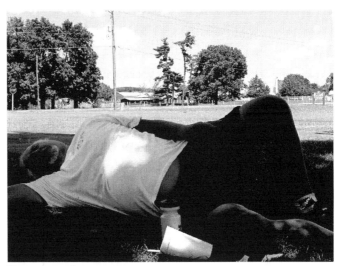

Down and out

Wipeouts Make Good Stories

Over time, I've had my share of wipeouts on
the road, one or two of them fairly dramatic,
most affecting my dignity more than my body
parts. It's easy to feel like an idiot when you
come crashing to the ground for no apparent
reason. What was I thinking? Why didn't I see
that tree root? I should have been able to
catch myself before it was too late.

Wipeouts are sudden, take us by surprise,
cannot be predicted or anticipated, and are
humbling. I think it's fair to say that wipeouts
are universal. We all suffer them, whether or
not we choose to hit the road running. We
can say to ourselves, *I'm going to watch it.*
That's never going to happen to me again. We
can say it, think it, resolve not be so careless

and unaware, but good luck. There are no guarantees. It will probably happen again.

My most interesting crash and burn occurred at the eleven-mile-mark during the Duke City Half Marathon in Albuquerque, New Mexico. Most of the course was a nice, soft dirt path beside a river, a surface that was kind to my sore but slowly recovering Achilles tendon. But for the last couple of miles the course left the river path and became concrete. My theory is that the added impact of the hard surface was a big factor in my fall, splat, face down causing a gash in my right elbow. I was limping a little, nursing that tendon and probably not picking up my feet the way I should have been. Oh yes, there were lots of spectators who showed their concern, then watched me get up and resume running.

I was way too close to the finish line to quit. There was a good bit of blood dripping from my elbow, but there was no pain right then, at least not at the wound site. At the finish line, (I still managed to win my age group.) they cleaned me up in the medical tent and my friend took me off to get stitches and an antibiotic. I healed fast. Elbow scars are insignificant.

I have tripped over tree roots running alone in the Maine woods where the ground is soft. I was glad there was no one around to see me fall flat.

Running along Mountain Avenue in downtown Fort Collins one day, I was admiring myself in a plate glass window and was able to see the beginning of my ungainly descent onto the sidewalk. That one hurt, but I jumped up immediately and continued to run, hoping against hope that no one had seen my performance.

Once I experienced a series of four or five falls in a period of a few weeks, nearly all of them on dirt trails where the ground was rough. I was beginning to wonder if this falling was going to become a permanent condition, but for whatever reason, I finally moved beyond that scary phase.

I don't hesitate to go out for a run when the roads are icy or snow-covered, but I have learned to proceed with care. I've learned the hard way to take turns slowly and to avoid getting the least bit off balance which causes me to swerve. That, I've discovered, is when a slip or fall is most likely.

Avoiding wipeouts is impossible. I have decided that the best approach is to accept the inevitable and savor the falls that are bound to happen. They are events that make for good stories down the road after the wounds heal and dignity returns.

Choose them with care

The Importance of Socks

What about socks? There's a whole lot of time, attention and money directed toward selecting the right running shoe, but socks, well they're no big deal—or are they?

Experienced runners care about their socks and every runner and walker will have happier experiences on the road or trail if they choose their socks with care. It only takes one bad sock to ruin a run.

If it's worn out or fits poorly, it can encourage blisters. If it has lost its elasticity and slips down into a runner's heel, it can irritate and cause pain. If it's too thick, it constricts, too thin and toes may freeze.

A look into the history of socks reveals that the first ones were made from animal skins gathered up and tied around the ankles. A little later, the ancient Greeks used matted

animal hair to cover their feet. Romans
preferred leather or woven fabrics. By 1000
AD socks had become a symbol of wealth.

By the fifth century, socks called "puttees"
were worn by holy men as a symbol of purity.
The invention of the knitting machine in
1589 meant that socks could be mass-
produced. By 1938 the invention of nylon
allowed socks to be made with a blend of
either wool, silk or cotton combined with
nylon, increasing durability.

In 2011, Datang, China, also known as "sock
city," produced eight billion pairs of socks,
enough for every person in the world to have
a pair.

Feet are the body's heaviest producers of
sweat emitting up to a half cup of liquid a day
from 250,000 eccrine sweat glands in each
foot. Probably that's why feet are so
notoriously smelly. Good socks can help by
absorbing sweat and helping it evaporate.

Wool absorbs 30 percent of its weight in
water and its anti-microbial properties cut
down on odor. High tech materials such as
lycra and polyester are also good for
absorbing and dispersing moisture.

Today's socks come in all shapes, lengths,
sizes, colors, styles, thicknesses and
combinations of materials. It's no longer
nerdy to wear a pair that doesn't match; in
fact it can be a fashion statement.

Over-the-ankle socks bridge the gap
between pant leg and shoe. Socks cushioned
at the forefoot and heel provide padding and
protect sensitive areas of the feet from the

shock of pounding. Elastic bands around the arch and ankle and spandex cuffs help keep socks in place. Left and right socks match the contours of each foot and provide a better fit. Some socks feature a tight reinforced weave in the arch area to improve support.

Toe socks, like gloves for your feet, isolate toes to prevent friction and protect callouses during long runs. Compression socks improve blood circulation, help stabilize joints and muscles, reduce risk of injury and promote stability and a sense of security for runners.

Take good care of your running socks. Wear them only to run or walk. Dirty ones increase the likelihood of blisters. Wash them inside-out to fluff the inside padding. Don't use bleach. Extend the life of your socks by using fabric softener and allowing them to air dry. Repurpose them when they begin to lose their shape.

Sock selection has become so complex that REI sporting goods store has "foot information specialists" to help customers with their sock choices.

The nice thing about socks is that they wear out within a year or so, making certain that when you give a gift of socks, they will always be welcome.

A Little Bit to Make You Fit

A genius of a name. It rhymes. It's short. It says it all. And for many, it is a "must have" item if you're serious about maximizing movement in your life. Or to be more accurate, if you are serious about recording your activity minute-by-minute including: the steps you take, the distance you cover, the calories you ingest, your heart rate, how well and how much you sleep, the number of "active" minutes you spend in a day, what time it is, your BMI, the weight you lose and the muscle mass you gain. I've probably missed a few things like caller ID, music control and GPS tracking-- but you get the idea.

I've heard that a FitBit can tell you when you're sick—even what is the matter with you, but I haven't verified those claims. Some models give you feedback—they smile at you when you do something right. They can sync automatically with your phone, IPad and computer or Bluetooth so wherever you are, whatever you are doing, you can be in touch with your body.

Warning: Choosing a Fitbit is no easy task. That "FitBit" word is the name for a whole family of fitness products designed to keep you motivated and improve your health by keeping track of your everything.

Described as "wearable technology," most of them are worn on your wrist, but you can find models that attach to a bra or T-shirt if wearing it on your wrist is just too much of a constant reminder of what you are or are not doing or should or should not be doing moment by moment.

You're gonna need a bit of cash if you want to own a FitBit. You can buy a "Zip" model for 59.95, a "One" for 99.95, a "Flex" for 99.95, a "Charge" for 129.95, a Charge HR" for 149.95 or a "Surge" for 249.95. Various models are classified as suitable for "everyday," "active," or "performance," wear. That must mean that you need more than one if you plan to track your daily activity, your active moments and any competitive events you enter. Should you be into tracking your weight, check into the "Aria Scale," a gizmo that lets you step on it to weigh yourself.

Surprisingly, the FitBit was not the first product of its kind. Forerunners include apps like Apple Healthkit and Google Fit, Microsoft Band, Apple Watch, Android Gear, MyFitnessPal, RunKeeper and EveryMove.

FitBits can energize one's competitive instinct. One hospital issued FitBits to all staff and employees and challenged them to "outFit" each other. A nurse moved into the lead by attaching his FitBit to the collar of his hyperactive dog. Another ran hers through the washing machine. It survived and she emerged as head of the pack.

Libby James

What happens if you wear two FitBits? Can you double your fitness along with your fun? Just wondering.

Hey! No wisecracks intended. I just think it is possible to get and stay fit without a tracker on your wrist.

Are You an Athlete?

A few days ago my daughter Kristin asked me a question. "Do you think of yourself as an athlete?"

I had an urge to seek a definition of the word from Google before I answered her but the Google dude was not immediately available so I was on my own.

I had to say, "No."

Then I asked, "Do you think of yourself as an athlete?" She took less time than I did to answer, "No."

Both of us have been physically active for a long time. She was a swimmer and tennis player in high school and has been hitting the running trails for at least three decades. She has done more than a dozen marathons and more half marathons than she can count. She has been a dedicated and consistent stretcher and weight-lifter for long enough that she has beautiful rippling muscles in her arms and legs to show for it.

I'm getting a little ancient for this running game, but I've been at it for a few years longer than Kristin has and I plan to do it for as long as I'm able. A run in the morning makes my day.

So. Why don't either of us see ourselves as athletes? What is an athlete anyway? I did go to the Google-dude and here's what I learned.

"An athlete is a person who is proficient in sports and other forms of exercise. Synonyms are "sportsman, sportswoman, sportsperson, jock, Olympian, runner."

Checking on the word "athlete" the old way—in a paper dictionary, I learned that athlete is derived from the French, *athlein,* to contend for a prize. The meaning is listed as "a person who is trained or skilled in exercises, sports or games requiring physical strength, agility or stamina."

Neither of us has ever had a coach or trainer but that does not mean that we have not trained. Runners like to talk about going on "training runs," which means that they are practicing—no doubt for the next race coming up on their schedule. We both do that but more often than not, we go out to run despite, wind, rain and cold, just because we like to. It makes us feel good. It is a time to think, a time to chat, a time to take a look around at the world and see what is going on.

I do remember being quite surprised a few years ago when someone said to me, "You look like a runner." I liked hearing that. I hadn't thought much about what a runner looks like, but I was happy to fit the image, at least in the eyes of one person.

Maybe Kristin and I don't think of ourselves as athletes because neither of us have dedicated the major portion of our lives to the act of running. I for one, have a hard time getting into the technicalities, though I am quite fascinated with the people who do. And it would probably help my running if I paid more attention to specific exercises, techniques, and recommended training schedules.

So. Do you think of yourself as an athlete? Would you choose to be one? Does it matter at all what words we use to define ourselves?

It's something to think about.

A favorite book about running

The Elements of Effort

I often turn to a little book by John Jerome called *The Elements of Effort*. Not only is it a favorite book about running, it has a whole lot to say about life in general. Sub-titled "reflections on the art and science of running," the author has organized the book by the seasons as he reflects on his favorite sport.

Of running he says in the introduction: "Running is the most elemental sport there is. We are genetically programmed to do it. One might even say that we are the free-ranging, curious, restless creatures that we are because of running. Surely our instinct for freedom is a legacy of this essential mobility. I think freedom itself is the source of running's great appeal. Slip on a pair of shoes, slip out the door, and you're there: free... Try though the gimmick-sellers have to complicate the sport, nothing has compromised running's essential simplicity."

John Jerome dedicates his book to the memory of Jim Fixx, author of the *Complete Book of Running*, who was responsible for getting so many runners started.

Here are some of Jerome's words of wisdom.

"Running—or any other effortful gross-motor activity, extended over time—is a powerful tool for keeping ourselves in the present tense, and the present tense is always a vacation."

"I've noticed that when a run gets tough I say to myself: 'Just be in the present moment and place, right here and now. Don't look ahead. Don't anticipate being finished. Just keep running.'"

"I'm happy using running for purposes other than longevity. I use it to set my body whirling, and thereby still my head."

"Seems to me, longevity is not the issue, maintaining a life that is satisfying and useful is the whole point. And who is not interested in stilling their incessant thinking machine and setting their body whirling—slow as it might be?"

"In masters (over age 40) athletics what most people master first is the art of ignoring the obvious: how old they are. (We're not going to let that stop us.) We become masters at carrying on, at persevering, at getting in our mileage and getting through our races, come hell or high water. To do so, we've had to build up a fairly heavy coating on our pain sensors. It's not easy to catch your body's subtle signals when you are essentially a callus from head to foot."

Amen to this one, I say. After a few weeks of walking instead of running because my body was complaining, I finally told it to shut up. I was going to run—at least down to that blue car. And when I got there, I kept going until I had circled the cemetery a mile from my house and run back home. Yep. It hurt. Yep. It felt wonderful!

"Aging is a disease of hypokinesis, a word that means lack of movement," according to John Jerome.

I believe it. It doesn't matter much what you do, as long as you get up and do it. And with consistency. The older we get, the harder it is to get back to working out if you lay off for more than a couple of days.

Another Jerome gem: "Breathing is life's single most sustainable activity. And it is breath itself that is so enhanced by running."

Breathe deep. Stay in the moment. Walk or run or bike or swim every day that you can manage it. And when you need a little inspiration, read a few words from John Jerome's book.

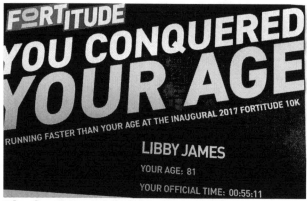

The first annual, held in Fort Collins,
September 2017

Fortitude

I had a pretty cool experience on Labor Day
2017. The organizers of the Bolder Boulder,
my all-time favorite 10k, brought Fortitude, a
10k road race with all the Bolder Boulder
trimmings, to Fort Collins for the first time
ever. Even better, the race went right past
the home where my children grew up, a
daughter's house, and the house where I live
now.

It was a weird and wonderful sensation. I
felt as if I was running in the Bolder Boulder,
as I have done so many times, but in this
totally familiar location. To make it even
better, Kristin, my older daughter, joined me
from Cheyenne for the run.

And Donna Messenger, one of the fastest
female runners in Fort Collins when she lived
here years ago, came from her home in Coeur
d' Alene, Idaho to run in the race. It was old
times revisited for her as well.

The course began just west of the Colorado State University campus and wound through neighborhoods until it returned to the campus and finished on the Sonny Lubick Field in the brand new, as yet unnamed, CSU football stadium. Runners circled the track inside the state-of-the-art structure to reach the finish line.

There were nearly 8,000 participants, making it by far the largest running event ever held in the Choice City. What a kick it was to see so many people circling a good part of the town encouraged by spectators and lively music from several bands along the way. Okay. So there was no sign of Bolder Boulder's famous fryers of bacon and belly dancers along the route, but just give it a year or two!

Elite runners took part in a handicapped "chase" race later in the morning, geared to making it possible for all the elites to arrive at the finish line at about the same time.

After they finished, citizen runners found seats to watch the elites enter the stadium and run around the track. There was a Labor Day ceremony celebrating first responders. Race organizers even thought to put a request for donations to the survivors of the recent Houston, Texas flood on the big screen in the stadium. Heads up to them!

Now I have two favorite 10ks, the Bolder Boulder that opens the season on Memorial Day and the Fortitude that ends the summer running season on Labor Day. Having two superbly organized races bracketing the

Still Running

season is a real bonus for those in search of a quality 10k.

Libby James

An adventure begins

Walking Coast to Coast

The age-old business of putting one foot in front of the other to propel oneself forward in pursuit of survival in the form of food, shelter, clothing, companionship; it's been going on since humans emerged on this earth.

And then we got mechanized. We didn't have to move so far and so fast under our own steam to survive, so we turned to other pursuits that often did not involve putting one foot in front of the other to fulfill our needs. But something was missing. Seems we need to move our bodies if we are to keep ourselves healthy and happy.

We have learned that putting one foot in front of the other satisfies that need to move.

Still Running

According to a whole raft of studies, we've learned that we will live longer, be happier, more shapely, mentally sharper, less wrinkled, better sleepers and have stronger bones, less stress, increased energy and more efficient immune systems if we'll only get out and move, first one foot and then the other, in some sort of forward motion.

Some of us run, others walk and some have discovered that a combination of the two works best for them. During more than four decades of running, I hadn't given much thought to walking. I've hiked quite a bit, and I walk—to the neighbor's house—to town to do an errand--but I don't plan "to walk," or at least I didn't until I participated in an 85-mile, six-day journey on the Coast-to-Coast path across the western half of northern England in 2015.

I did train some for that walk but my rambles around town and in the nearby foothills weren't really adequate preparation for this venture. The word "path" conjured up a gentle stroll across the British countryside for me, something the hilly, rock-strewn course of the Coast-to-Coast is definitely *not*. I have new respect for the Brits and their "walks."

In this part of the world, mountains are called fels and during the course of this walk, we encountered a few hardy "fels runners" looking incredibly nimble and at home in the steep, rough territory they were traversing. I questioned it when someone told me that members of the first Everest expedition had trained in these hills, but now I get it.

There was no time during the walk that I had a desire to break into a run. The terrain was too steep and rocky. Human beings, even those who have not trained much, can walk for a long time before they tire. We're bio-engineered that way. But by the end of a day ranging from 14 to 21 miles, feet become sore and fatigue sets in. The sensation is different from the pain that emerges deep into a long run or a race; not as intense but equally persistent until it's time to stop.

After doing the first 85 miles of the 191-mile Coast-to-Coast walk, I was ready to return and tackle the rest of it. I embarked on this part of the journey with a new respect for the art of walking and an enduring appreciation for the opportunity to meet fellow walkers and have enough breath to get to know them as the miles pass.

In 2017, largely the same congenial group of seven returned to complete the Coast-to-Coast path.

I could have marked off a 108-mile path starting from my house. I could have walked to Estes Park and home again. It would have been: very convenient, easy to plan and pay for, and would have involved absolutely no hassle on busses, trains and planes to arrive at the starting point. And the exercise/fresh air component would have been similar.

But no. It would never have measured up to our 108-mile jaunt through Yorkshire on the Coast-to-Coast path. Here are some reasons why.

The scenery—green, green, green; the farm fields dotted with grazing cows and baaing, shaggy sheep giving you the eye as you make your way through a never-ending series of gates, stiles and fences. The stone walls that have been standing for eons with no mortar to hold them together, the ingenuity of those who had to do something with the endless rocks that needed to be removed before fields could be farmed. The walls mark oddly-shaped fields and seem to have no rhyme or reason as they stretch across the hillsides. Then there are the crumbling edifices of the past such as the enormous remains of Eastby Abbey in Richmond, a bustling market town of 8,400. It was there that we rendezvoused with special relatives and enjoyed a dizzying array of delicious dishes at an Indian restaurant.

About the food. One member of our group gained almost five pounds, only partially the result of "full English breakfasts" that started with a choice of fruit, yogurt, granola or cold cereal and progressed to eggs, bacon, sausage, baked beans, tomatoes, toast and blood pudding (which we all passed on). You could choose to try a kipper for breakfast for some variety. Pub dinner favorites were fish and chips and steak and ale or chicken pie. And then there was the beer, which became a necessity at the end of each day. The English do an amazing job of food presentation—it always looks so good—so beautifully arranged on the plate.

The second part of the path, from Kirkby Stephen to Robin Hood's Bay is a bit less rocky, steep and wild than the first half from St. Bees to Kirkby Stephen, but it has its own challenges. There's a 24-mile day, mostly flat, and a 13-mile day where you climb up to a summit and down the other side on narrow, rocky paths four times, always thinking that this hill will surely be the last one. Knees and toes object to the steep downs. The Brits tend to stepping stones rather than switchbacks. They are so tough. The peat bogs were a challenge, making for wet, muddy feet, but not as bad as they might have been in wet weather. We experienced only a single hour of rain on the entire trip. Hours after we finished, the skies clouded up and the rain began.

And the people: A highlight for me was walking for a whole day with Mark Rushworth and his wife, Debbie. Mark is a Yorkshire lad who lived with our family in 1976 and attended high school with my children. We've been friends ever since, and always will be. We met Mark and his family in a campsite in Germany, in pouring down rain when Mark was 11. His mother, Pat, joined the group for dinner and the evening and gave a little talk about this long-time friendship that brought a tear to my eye.

These are a few of the things I would not have experienced walking close to home. I don't mind putting up with crowded airports, delayed planes, luggage hauling, security lines and sleepless hours in the air. While it is always good to be home, I'd go again, even tomorrow. I hope that I never forget the exhilaration of getting away, being in a new place, and meeting interesting people.

Libby James

Arndt, Lee, and James families ready to run

Thanksgiving Day Run

Some forty-five-hundred humans plus uncounted numbers of dogs and strollers turned out for a four-mile jaunt starting at 9 a.m. in downtown Fort Collins on Thanksgiving morning. Some of these humans were very fast and earned prize money for their efforts, but most ran because what better way is there to celebrate gratitude for family, friends, community and the anticipation of a great feast later in the day?

Members of my family have been participating in the race on Thanksgiving Day morning since some of the grandkids were young enough to ride in a stroller. This year two daughters, two sons-in-law and four grandkids showed up at my house ready to run. No one had to be coerced to do it!

207

Cool sunny weather with enough wind to make runners take notice was the order of the day for this race, the largest in Northern Colorado at the time. From the start on College Avenue, the main street of town, the route took runners west for a mile-plus, then around City Park Lake to make a loop and head east back to the downtown finish line on College Avenue.

After the race, there was time for participants and spectators to meet up with friends. Everyone seemed animated and happy to see each other and catch up with the latest goings on.

At the awards ceremony there were cash prizes for the overall winners and big beautiful pies for age group winners. By late morning, the crowds had dwindled. People were headed home to get on with the holiday festivities.

A morning run is a good way to start any day and, to my way of thinking, the very best way to get ready for a memorable Thanksgiving Day.

Libby James

Barbara and Stu Krebs arrive out of the night

Winter Wilderness Adventure

The sun was shining. The air was crispy cold
on this Wednesday morning in January.
There was a slight breeze at 11,350 feet but
my hands and feet were warm—actually
warm! As we headed down the hill, my
backpack was significantly lighter than it had
been two days earlier when, one plodding
snowshoed foot at a time, with frequent
pauses to catch my breath, I arrived at the
Broome Hut on the Second Creek drainage in
the Vasquez Peak Wilderness area.

Described as "a jewel between Berthoud
Pass and Winter Park," in the Rocky
Mountains, the Broome Hut exists as a labor
of love that took 15 years to build. It
replaced a dilapidated A-frame built in the
1950s. Actual construction took two-and-a-
half years preceded by a long and tedious

time obtaining the necessary permits and raising $400,000. Dozens of helicopter flights deposited half a million pounds of materials in the remote area and volunteers donated 6,000 hours of labor.

The trailhead to this incredibly beautiful spot begins three miles from Berthoud Pass on the Winter Park side and winds just under a mile with an elevation gain of about 800 feet, to the hut perched above treeline. Four bedrooms sleep 16 in bunks. The hut has photovoltaic lighting, a wood pellet stove, two composting toilets, an expansive common area, and kitchen complete with two sinks, two propane stove tops, a water pump and a full set of dishes and utensils. Perhaps the most wonderful feature is the huge windows that look out upon a pristine cirque with snowy cornices and chutes below an avalanche-prone ridge.

Backcountry skiers approach this paradise with caution carrying shovels, probes and avalanche beacons, and always with a buddy. I was part of a group of 16 that included a dozen seasoned backcountry skiers and a smaller contingent of older outdoorsy types who navigated the trail on snowshoes.

For well over two decades, this group has done an annual trip to one of the Tenth Mountain Division ski huts located in the Rocky Mountains roughly between Crested Butte, Breckenridge, Leadville and Vail. The group has varied over the years but being part of it has remained a goal for anyone who has ever done one of these trips. It takes a good bit of planning, beginning as long as a year before a trip occurs, when the highly sought after huts must be reserved.

Dian Sparling of Fort Collins, whose sons were raised on cross-country skis, orchestrated the trip details for many years and now has help from her friends, Meegan Flenniken and Eric Odell. They issue invitations, collect fees and assign food groups.

Over time, traditions have developed. We play the same silly games every year. The menu doesn't change much. Groups are assigned to bring breakfast or dinner and everyone is on their own for lunch. Appetizers and drinks are plentiful, all hauled up the mountain on the backs of the skiers.

Every year Stu Krebs, of Montrose, Colorado, who, at 83 lays claim to being the oldest among us, asks each person to share a bit about their relationship with the group and how and when they joined. That always gets the conversation going.

There's ample time for playing in the snow, practicing intricate techniques for the hot shot skiers, and for reading, napping, gazing out the window, engaging in leisurely conversation, and sensing the serenity of the natural world away from everyday concerns for a couple of days.

After a dramatic sunset, a satisfying dinner and a few games of farkel, tenzi or "hands" around a long table, bedtime usually comes early.

Stu impressed us all by creating a basket
for a ski pole with a beer can lid, a bit of wire
and his amazing ability to fix anything. We'll
also remember three of us who doubled the
distance of our trip up the hill by tromping up
the wrong drainage for almost a mile before
we met a skier who told us we were not
where we were supposed to be. We'll
remember not being able to use the facilities
on top of Berthoud Pass. They were locked
and the area was not ploughed out because of
a government shutdown. Apparently toilets
are not considered essential by officialdom.

What we will all remember is the
camaraderie that we felt more strongly than
ever this year, that seems to grow and
deepen as time passes and the traditions
become ever more precious.

Libby James

Cougar James airborne

A Race with the Boys

It took Cougar, my skinny 14-year-old grandson and me 52 minutes and 35 seconds to make it around the 5k course at City Park near my home in Fort Collins on our first, and what turned out to be our only, training run. We jogged and walked, jogged and walked, and before we were through Cougar was more interested in playing with a set of little magnetic balls he pulled out of his pocket than he was with completing the distance. But he made it. The first time he'd ever done 3.1 miles

That was mid-week. On Saturday morning Cougar and I, plus his brother, Drogin, 17, a /football/basketball/baseball player, lined up at the start of the 5k Run for Hope. Joining us were two more of my grandsons. Henry 16, the reader/computer whiz/ World War II historian, and his brother, Mason, 14, soccer and Frisbee player who spends part of every day working out.

There were all sorts of predictions. How many of them would beat the old lady? And by how much? Would everyone finish? This race is so close to home that sneaking off part-way through the course was an option I did not mention to them. Whining was a possibility, too, but who would be there to hear it? I for sure, wasn't going to hang back to listen.

But none of that happened. Cougar took off like a shot, keeping up with Mason and Drogin for a good 100 yards. I saw him stop, panting, at the side of the road. "Walk a little and catch your breath," I called to him.

I didn't see any of the boys again. After I finished, I ran back to encourage Henry up the final hill. There were some strange and ominous sounds coming out of him, but he didn't stop running until he crossed the finish line in 37 minutes.

And then came Cougar, arms and legs flip-flopping all over the place. By the time he crossed the finish line, he'd cut 10 minutes off his practice time and there was a huge smile on his face. He had so much fun that when it came time to go home, he ran the whole way.

Mason beat us all, finishing in 20:30, fourth place among a competitive group of 13-15-year-old boys. What might he have done if he'd trained?

Grandsons Mason, Drogin, and Henry

Drogin's 22:45 was good enough for first place in 16-19 boys and earned him an iconic T.S. Berger ceramic pot. He doesn't yet know what a treasure that is.

Granny did 24:27, the only person in her age group. They skipped announcing the 70 and over category in the paper. Oh well. But it would have been nice to save that small print as evidence that I was lucky enough to run a 5k with four grandsons on August 4, 2012.

Estelle and Roger Hahn with their houseguest at Festival of Races, 2016

Big Welcome in Syracuse

From Fort Collins, Colorado to Syracuse, New York. That's a long way to go to run in a three-mile race, but I can't think of a better reason to take to the cramped and crowded airways than to take part in the 24th running of the Festival of Races 5k Masters Championships in 2016. The weekend ranked right up there with the best running experiences I've ever had.

It was my great good fortune to stay with Estelle and Roger Hahn, long-time dedicated runners who not only opened up their beautiful home to me, but even picked me up at the airport. During my time there, we enjoyed delicious meals and stimulating conversation together. We became friends.

On Saturday morning, Estelle and I hobnobbed with other runners as we picked up our race packets at Dick's Sporting Goods. Seems like the older runners get, the more they become committed to their sport and to the welfare of their fellow runners. They love to chat about past experiences, injuries and other disasters and stats and predictions about the upcoming event. Who's coming? Who isn't? What will the weather be like?

Sunday, race day, dawned cloudy but dry, to everyone's delight. The temperature was in the 60s, there was no wind and only a tiny bit of humidity for a spoiled Coloradan to whine about.

This race was low altitude for me, coming from 5,000 feet, which meant more available oxygen, an advantage that might allow me a faster time than I could do at home. I had turned 80 a few months before the race and therefore was in a new age group hoping to run the course in under 25 minutes.

By the time I reached the 1k mark and looked at my watch, I was fairly sure that was not going to happen. I was right. I finished in a gun time of 25:14, chip time 25:11, a few seconds slower than the time I'd been shooting for. (Gun time begins when the gun goes off. Chip time is the actual time it takes from stepping over the start line to arriving at the finish line.) Turned out that 25.14 was good enough for an American record, surpassing a time that had stood for 27 years.

Estelle took third in her 75-79 age group, beaten out by her friend Fran who crossed the finish line at exactly the same time as Estelle did. In a "photo finish" the camera showed that Fran's torso had crossed the finish line before Estelle's did. Estelle, who has done 23 of the 24 Festival 5k races, will be sticking her chest out a bit more the next time she runs the race.

Libby James

Shamrock 8k, Virginia Beach

Hot Irish stew at the finish line.

That was a first for me and mighty welcome
as I completed the Shamrock 8k road race in
Virginia Beach on St Patrick's Day in 2018.
The course was a flat, sea-level, out-and-back
along the edge of the Atlantic Ocean. It was
cool and breezy enough that the stew really
hit the spot.

There are moments, as I prepare for a race,
from plunking down the money for lodging
and plane fare to the hassle of travel, that I
wonder why I'm doing all this. There's
nothing to get nervous about, yet I still have a
hard time sleeping the night before a race—
crazy! The moment I line up at the start,
suddenly it is all worthwhile and I wonder
why I ever thought otherwise.

More than 7,000 people ran this race, the
first event in a weekend that included kids'
races and a half and full marathon the
following day. Off-season in Virginia Beach is
the perfect time to stage such an enormous
event. The hotels and restaurants are
plentiful and there's a state-of-the-art
convention center to hold packet pick-up, an
expo and a slate of speakers. A Hilton Hotel a
few steps from the start has to be one of the
most comfortable places ever to stay warm
during the moments before a race.

Sixteen "corrals" kept the runners separated according to predicted times and staggered their starts so that the narrow boardwalk never seemed crowded. Everywhere runners celebrated St. Patrick's Day with lots of "wearing of the green."

Being part of the USATF (track and field organization) made this huge race seem small and intimate. The USATF participants lined up in corral number one, right on the start line. A separate awards ceremony was held following the race for the USATF competitors, who came from all across the country. Old friendships were renewed and there was the usual chatter about upcoming races and dealing with injuries. Runners are such a congenial crowd, it is a pleasure to interact with them.

I can't think of a better way to spend a weekend.

Cousins cheer on Abby, the runner, NY
marathon, 2017

Abby's First Marathon

More than 50,000 people were nursing sore
muscles the next day. They're the ones who
ran 26.2 miles through New York's five
boroughs during the 47th running of the New
York Marathon on November 5, 2017

The event began in 1970 when, of 127
entrants on a course entirely in Central Park,
55 men finished and the sole woman entrant
dropped out. Entry fee was $1 and the entire
budget for the race was $1,000. The now
iconic race has blossomed into a mammoth
exercise in community spirit and a symbol of
hope and renewal. It was held less than two
months after the 9/11 attacks in 2001. In
2017 the race went on shortly after another
tragic event that caused increased police

presence throughout the race. The only time the race was cancelled was in 2012 because of Hurricane Sandy. That year runners showed their support by running together in Central Park on race day.

Among those resting up after the marathon was my 24-year-old granddaughter, Abby, who finished with a smile on her face and surrounded by a gaggle of her cousins who had come to cheer her on. She had never run more than 17 miles at a time before, but she chalked up more than 26 miles with no problem. She and I did one of her very first runs, 20 minutes around a small lake, when she was a teenager. She has come a long way, baby, and who knows where she may go from here.

Libby James

Joan Benoit and Libby in Albany, 2017

Two Races Age Up in 2018

Two of my favorite running races, the
Freihofer's 5k for Women in Albany, New
York and the Bolder Boulder 10k in Boulder,
Colorado turned forty within days of each
other in the spring of 2018.

In 2012 I was a newbie at Freihofer's,
surrounded by elite women runners gathered
from all around the world for the 34th
running of this famous all-women's race
made possible by the sponsorship of an old
and very generous New England bakery. I
was the oldest invited athlete by 20 years and

the only novice. These women chattered about the technicalities of running non-stop and I soaked up every word in the hospitality suite that has been provided for us in the Hotel Albany.

I learned about Olympic Trials, the difference between certified, sanctioned, and validated courses, the dietary benefits of blueberries, and the nagging injuries that plague these women who devote themselves so completely to their sport.

I was unabashedly in awe, thrilled to be in the same room with them. For someone who never ran a race until age 40 and didn't own a pair of racing flats until three-plus years ago, what am I doing here?

I heard about their demanding travel schedules, selecting races, juggling work and families, and intense training. These women routinely run twice a day and think nothing of getting up in the middle of the night to make it happen—and to get their kids off to school on time as well. I met the race organizers, a few paid, most not, who tend to the thousands of details that go into organizing a race and supporting these elite participants. "Coach" Jim, looking every inch a runner, cracked jokes and made sure we knew how to get to the start, find the elite area, and understand the quirks of the course so that we can do our best.

My roommate—another stroke of luck for me—was Sheri Piers of Falmouth, Maine who, along with full-time work as a nurse practitioner, has three pre-teen children, and just incidentally was the first American woman finisher in the 2012 Boston Marathon.

We hit it off immediately. Sheri hates 5ks. She calls them barn burners. "They hurt so much," she says. "I prefer the slow roast of a marathon where there's some wiggle room. In a 5k, one small mistake and that's that. No chance to redeem yourself."

After a morning spent talking to children in area schools, the invited runners gathered for a press conference. There was a line-up of TV cameras and reporters, words from the race director, and from Joan Benoit Samuelson. She's a lady I'd hoped to meet ever since I did her signature 10k Beach to Beacon run in Maine three years earlier. At 55, she was older than all the other elite masters (over 40) women with a single obvious exception. This running icon who won the first Olympic women's marathon in 1984, not only spoke with great warmth and sincerity, she steamed through the 5k course in 18:23.

It was impossible not to have a major case of jitters prior to this prestigious run. I was happy to learn that Sheri got nervous too, before every race. A predicted rainstorm downgraded to a warm drizzle as we began to run. Mamitu Daska of Ethiopia held her early lead for the entire race, winning in 15:19.

I tried to take advantage of the downhills, stretching out my stride. It *hurt.* It also felt great. My 23:34 was good for dead last among the elites, but a first in terms of pure enjoyment for me--an event for the books.

Fast forward three years and I was back in Albany for the 37th running of Freihofers. I'd arrived in Albany late Thursday night, having finished the 37th running of the Bolder Boulder three days before.

Both races are community festivals in the very best sense of that concept. I think that's why they have endured and prospered over so many years. It is also because of a core of dedicated race organizers and volunteers who work all year long tending to the thousands of preparatory details required to make these events successful. And where would the races be without the commitment of loyal sponsors who return year after year to provide funding?

Both races draw elite runners from all over the world. They make significant commitments to non-profits, and these days, because they have been around for so long, the races have become must-do events for many.

John Tope of Denver, elite runner recruiter for Freihofers, is an example. Before he left for Albany, he *had* to run the Bolder Boulder because he's done every single one of them. Despite the fact that he injured his Achilles tendon at mile one, he *had* to hobble through the entire race or face the ending of an era. As a result, he gimped around at Freihofer's, protecting his foot with a borrowed boot about five sizes too small with his toes sticking out the end as he attended to the needs of the elite runners.

This year I arrived in Albany in time to visit Southgate Elementary School on Friday morning. More than 100 highly energetic fourth, fifth and sixth graders greeted me. I told them about writing a middle-grade novel called *Running Mates.* "How many races have you run?" One kid asked.

"I have no idea," I replied. "I can tell you that I have been racing for 39 years, about 15 to 18 races a year. You do the math. A few minutes later, a boy in the middle of the room piped up. "I did the math," he said proudly. Some questions were tougher. "If you had to choose between running and writing, which would you choose?" Given the circumstances and the moment, I had to say running.

The Freihofers race draws 4,000 women every year. In the Bolder Boulder, more than 50,000 souls take off in waves staggered over a two-and-a-half hour period, to tour the city of Boulder on their feet and finish in the University of Colorado Football Stadium. The elite runners start later and run a separate race that also ends in the stadium, now filled with citizen runners cheering the elites to the finish line.

The Albany race goes past the stately New York State Capitol Building and swings through a shady Washington Park before returning to the starting area. There are mother-daughter, grandmother-mother-daughter, sister-sister and family-and-friends teams, corporate teams, club teams and a big contingent of women who had been training for 10 weeks to run their first 5k race.

In Albany, Nancy Gerstenberger, 85, running in her hometown race, completed the course in one hour five minutes, 24 seconds. It took Emily Chebet of Kenya, 15 minutes and 38 seconds to cover the same ground. Both winners. I have travelled across the country for six years in a row to run a very special 3.1 mile race. I can't resist returning to this event even though it falls so soon after Memorial Day and the running of the Bolder Boulder 10k.

Gone Running

One night I decided to change the burned out light bulb in the ceiling above the center of my bed. I'd been putting it off because I have to stand on the bed and reach up as high as I can to remove the heavy glass shade and replace the bulb. A mattress isn't the steadiest surface to balance on. I wondered for a moment if I was still tall enough to complete this task. (People shrink as they get older, you know.) Silly me. It hadn't been *that* long since the bulb had needed changing. Mission accomplished with a shaky moment or two but no disaster.

But in the process, I caught sight of a humungous layer of dust all across the top of my tall wardrobe. An accumulation of who knows how many years. Choking in the dust was a jewelry box, a pink piggy bank, several family photos and a small stand-up sign that read **GONE RUNNING.** I think *Runners World* magazine once gave these signs away.

That's it, I thought in the middle of the night! That's what I'd like people to say about me when all is said and done. Surely a hilly, wooded trail awaits somewhere in the sky. I think I'd better obey that sign.

The next day was Saturday and I went to the foothills and ran for 10 miles. At mile nine, someone called out, "Libby."

"Who is it?" I asked, squinting into the sun.

"It's Libby," came the reply. It was Libby Hickman, Olympian, 1997 winner of the Bolder Boulder and *Runner's World* road

racer of the year three times, one of the best
runners Colorado has ever produced. Now a
home-schooling mother of three living in Fort
Collins, Libby doesn't compete much but runs
regularly and shares a fitness business with
her husband. They were out in the hills
running together. That's what I'll remember
about my run that day. Meeting up by chance
with Libby Hickman, a person and runner for
whom I have the greatest admiration. I love it
that we share the same name. Once, a small
article in our local paper about me was titled
"The Other Libby." I liked that!

On Sunday afternoon, the November
weather was so incredibly nice that I headed
for the hills again, this time for a leisurely
walk on a road overlooking the reservoir. At
the start I greeted three women walking and
chatting together. I slipped by them and soon
they were out of sight. On my return trip, I
ran into them again and said, "Hello again."

"You were fast," one of them said. "Did you
run to the dam?"

"No. But maybe I walked kind of fast
because I'm used to running.

"Are you Libby?"

"Yes."

"I'm Eileen."

"Oh my gosh, the sweet potato lady," I
exclaimed. "You look wonderful! You're a
miracle!"

"I am," she replied. I knew Eileen 20 years
ago when she was in the midst of a long-term
fight with cancer. When I substituted at the
elementary school where she taught, I got to

know her. Things didn't look good at the time, but in the end, she won the battle. What I remembered from all those years ago was her fierce concentration on diet and the fact that she swore by sweet potatoes. She made me a fan of them.

There she was on a rocky uphill slope, hiking with friends. No telling who you'll come across if you head out for the hills or around the lake, or onto the wooded path.

Put up a sign that says gone running and just do it.

Still Running

Acknowledgements

A big thank you to the loyal readers of my running column and blog for your interest, support, and for telling your stories. Thanks to everyone who has run with me, talked to me about running and inspired me through more than four decades to keep on running.

A special thanks to my granddaughter, Abby Arndt and to Gary Raham. I could not have managed without their technical skills.

24589509R00133

Made in the USA
Lexington, KY
17 December 2018